Nancy's
Healthy Kitchen
Baking Book

MACMILLAN • USA

Nancy's

Healthy Kitchen

BAKING BOOK

Nancy Fox

MACMILLAN • USA

MACMILLAN

A Simon & Schuster Macmillan Company
1633 Broadway
New York, NY 10019-6785

Library of Congress Cataloging-in-Publication Data

Fox, Nancy.
Nancy's healthy kitchen baking book / Nancy Fox.
p. cm.
Includes index.
ISBN 0-02-861587-5 (alk. paper)
1. Low-fat diet—Recipes. 2. Low-calorie diet—Recipes. 3. Desserts.
4. Baking. I. Title.
RM237.7.F69 1997   97-20885
641.5'638—DC21   CIP

ISBN: 0-02-861587-5

Manufactured in the United States of America

10 9 8 7 6 5 4 3 2 1

BOOK DESIGN BY KEVIN HANEK

Dedication

To the greatest husband, Allen, and sons, Evan and Charlie. I'm the luckiest person alive.

Contents

Acknowledgments

I owe the greatest debt to my husband, Allen, who collaborated with me on the writing, added beautiful and graphic descriptions of the desserts, and told my personal anecdotes better than I could have. He was also my most valuable taste tester, having been gifted with a discerning palate and penetrating honesty.

We would like to give a big kiss to our two sons, Evan and Charlie. They behaved like real troopers when, for over six months, we devoted most of our waking hours to this project. They also did a great job of taste testing, but they don't get too much credit for this because they had a ball eating everything in sight.

We also owe a great debt to our book agents, Maureen and Eric Lasher, who helped us choose the topic, structure, and writing style of the book.

I would also like to thank the most wonderful parents anyone could have, Roberta and Bob Novick, who made me believe that I could accomplish anything I set my mind to.

Finally, there is the Computrition Corporation of Chatsworth, which supplied me with their wonderful computer software system. This system was so simple and complete that it allowed me to calculate all the nutritional information I needed even though I am not particularly skillful with computers.

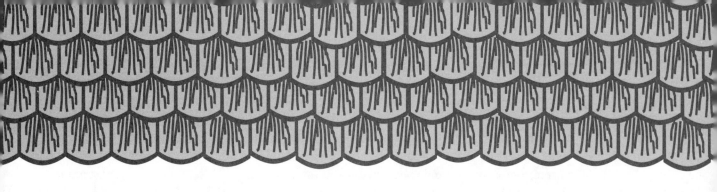

Introduction

Most of us want to eat healthy, nutritious foods, including desserts. And we're probably capable of denying ourselves the pleasures of the palate in order to experience the pleasures of slimmer waistlines, trimmer thighs, and the masochistic gratification that comes from Spartan eating.

But most of us cannot do this forever. We need treats. We long to follow up our meals with desserts that really taste good. At midmorning or midafternoon, when we start to run a little low on energy, we get the yen for something sweet and delicious to accompany a hot cup of coffee or a cold glass of milk. On quiet evenings at home when the family gathers for communal entertainment we can add excitement and life to the proceedings with a hot plate of freshly baked cookies or a batch of frosted muffins. When we are alone and bored we often feel the need for a tasty snack to fill the void.

The goal of this book is to allow everyone to enjoy great desserts without paying an exorbitant price in terms of calories or health.

In this cookbook I have compiled my best dessert recipes. Even though they are all low in fat and calories, they have the rich, decadent taste that people want. I love traditional American-style desserts that are easy to make, not fringy gourmet items. My favorites are fudgy brownies oozing rich chocolate, mouth-watering snickerdoodles and chocolate chip cookies hot from the oven, and thick creamy cheesecake. I also think you will be pleasantly surprised by the chapters on milkshakes and frozen desserts. These are items that the average person watching fat and calories probably never expected to eat or drink again.

What qualifies me to write this book and make these statements? Like most people, when I was a little girl I could eat anything I wanted. It was wonderful. I was skinny as a stick. In fact my sister used to say I looked like I had two pencils for legs and an eraser for a rear end. And I loved eating junk foods. In addition to eating regular foods, every day at school I stuffed myself with half a dozen chocolate chip cookies in the morning; grilled cheese, Swiss cookies, and chocolate milk at midmorning; and after lunch, I would stand in the candy lines and get a couple of candy bars and popcorn. After school I raided the cupboards for potato chips while waiting for the ice-cream truck to show up with sweets. Dinner was normal, but I always saved room for dessert. Although my mother and sister were overweight and always on some kind of diet, the thought of having to lose weight never entered my mind. And I thought it would go on forever.

I later learned that it wouldn't, but in the meantime I became deeply involved with rich desserts. I started baking at the age of nine, thanks to two inspiring grandmothers who were wonderful bakers. For years, I enjoyed creating decadent desserts for family and friends.

Having always been an entrepreneur at heart and, armed with a business degree, I started the first muffin and gift company in Los Angeles, called Mrs. Beasley's. This was in 1980, before muffins were commercially popular. I created new flavors, like pistachio and poppy seed, which were copied by other companies, and began baking minimuffins that were cute and bite-sized, an idea that also was copied. But the taste of Mrs. Beasley's was not commercial; we brought home baking to a retail market.

Mrs. Beasley's gifts consisted of fresh baked muffins, cookies, and brownies packed in beautiful baskets. These were hand-delivered to a customer list of entertainment celebrities and business people. Among Beasley's clients were Johnny Carson, Ed McMahon, Bette Midler, Rob Lowe, Michael Ovitz, Barbra Streisand, Dustin Hoffman, Neil Diamond, and Paramount, Disney, and Universal Studios. Several Beasley baskets were even sent to Ronald Reagan while he was president. After growing the business to three retail locations and one franchised location, I sold Mrs. Beasley's to an investment company in 1990.

But even before I sold Mrs. Beasley's my food interests had begun to change. As I moved into my twenties, I continued my childhood eating habits, but I started to notice a fair bit of unsightly swelling on the outside of my thighs and around my tummy. Incredible as it was, I was actually *getting fat*. I couldn't believe it. So that's what my sister and mom were talking about when they said, "Just wait until you get older. Like the rest of us, you'll have to watch your eating, too."

I had put on about fifteen pounds before I was convinced that I had to take action. I guess it was the new look in my boyfriend's eyes that finally did it. The "you are the most attractive little creature I have ever seen" look changed to a "it wouldn't hurt to take off a few pounds" look. That really hurt. And his subtle remarks like, "Are you sure you really want to eat that?" did not exactly pass unnoticed either. (If I had been a few years older and more worldly I would have gotten rid of the boyfriend along with the extra pounds.) But in any case, reality had struck. I was no longer a kid. Maybe that is the true mark of the passing of youth—it's gone when you can no longer eat anything you want.

So I started dieting. Having no experience with such things, I didn't know exactly where to begin, but simply cutting down my food intake had a decidedly unappealing ring. I tried it for a while, but I was constantly thinking of food. It is interesting how quickly a food obsession can develop. In most cases, as it did in my case, full blown food obsession appears about ten seconds after you first have to cut down on your eating because you are getting too fat. As soon as you discover that you can't eat whatever and whenever you want, you seem to spend an inordinate amount of time thinking about food.

So I tried a number of fancy diets that promised easy weight loss, and of course, none of them worked. The only method that really produced good long-term results was the boring old-fashioned method of consuming fewer calories. And cutting back on calories usually involved reducing fats, the most concentrated source of calories.

The foods were not a big problem, but the desserts were. At Mrs. Beasley's we were proud of the fact that we used plenty of farm fresh eggs, creamery butter, and the richest chocolate. It was easy to make great desserts when I had access to the richest ingredients. But with my changing personal needs these ingredients began to sound less and less good to me. It was becoming clear that cutting fat and calories made sense. But I was addicted to rich-tasting desserts and had difficulty going for even one day without them. And the commercial reduced-fat desserts simply did not taste good enough to satisfy me.

On top of that were the health concerns. I had married a wonderful man whose family had a terrible history of early heart disease. My husband was starting to experience some mild symptoms himself. It was nothing life threatening, but enough to frighten me into trying to improve his diet. High-fat desserts were a constant menace, and I could not rely on willpower alone to keep the situation under control. For both of our sakes and for the benefit of our two young children, Evan and Charlie, who share our genetic health risks but for whom willpower is a word they can neither understand nor spell, I needed to come up with dessert recipes that were low in fat but still good in taste, good enough to make eating desserts fun again.

I spent the next four years developing a wonderful variety of home-baked desserts that we could enjoy guilt-free. I got rave reviews from family, friends, and neighbors, but my best critics were Evan and Charlie, who had no concerns about fat or calories. They just wanted it to taste good. When they walked away from a plate of cookies after just one bite, I threw the cookies down the disposal and started again. When they came home from school with their friends and happily ate the desserts I had been testing that day, I knew I had a success!

After all the work I had put in to developing these great low-fat recipes, I wasn't content to use them only at home. I saw that there was a void in the market and that the recipes could be the basis for another business: Nancy's Healthy Kitchen, where the low-fat foods and desserts actually taste as good or better than their high-fat counterparts.

I opened Nancy's Healthy Kitchen in 1994 and it has been terrifically successful. It is actually three food businesses in one: (1) a low-fat restaurant and bakery with locations in Encino and Beverly Hills, California; (2) a line of packaged cookies that are marketed nationally through specialty retailers such as Neiman Marcus and Macy's and a host of smaller gourmet stores and markets; and (3) a line of gifts that are marketed nationally by catalogue. Our customers include Kirstie Alley, Dick Clark, Clint Black, Lisa Hartman, Howie Mandel, John Ritter, and Tom Arnold, to name-drop just a few. Our fresh low-fat baked goods, which are sold at our retail bakery, include muffins, cookies, cakes, quick breads, baked donuts with frosting, brownies, pies, and tortes.

Everyone wants low-fat and low-calorie desserts, but most commercial low-fat baked goods taste like Styrofoam. I strive for decadent taste first and foremost. The philosophy of Nancy's Healthy Kitchen is that everything must taste as good or better than the high-fat version (otherwise we will all ultimately blow it and splurge with Häagen-Dazs or McDonalds). You'll love the recipes in this book. And even though they rarely contain more than a few grams of fat per serving, they'll never leave you feeling deprived.

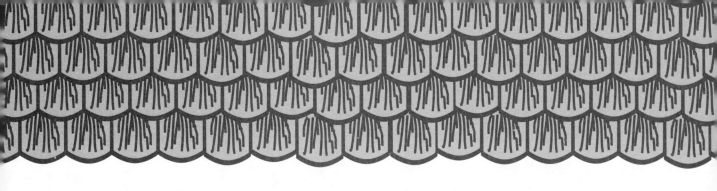

Ingredients

The following ingredients are particularly useful for low-fat and low-calorie baking. Fat is the prime culprit in high-calorie desserts because it is the most concentrated source of calories, not to mention being potentially harmful to your health. By reducing fat to the lowest levels consistent with good taste, we manage to reduce calories and the health risk at the same time. Sugar is also high in calories, but reducing both fat and sugar simultaneously is usually fatal to the taste of the dessert.

I will not describe here the low-fat ingredients that everyone is familiar with, such as flour, skim milk, and sugar. The following ingredients are some of the less common ones that will soon become staples in your refrigerator and pantry because they allow you to minimize fat while maintaining taste, moisture, and texture.

Fats and Fat Substitutes

Margarine:

Smart Beat margarine is one of my best finds for low-fat baking. I use it whenever possible because it has the lowest fat content per tablespoon (two grams) of any commercial margarine. It also contains no saturated fat. Unfortunately, it does not work in all baking situations. Often I have to combine it with other sources of fat to get the proper taste and texture, or simply use other margarines.

If Smart Beat doesn't work, I use reduced-fat margarine or regular corn oil margarine. Reduced-fat margarine is essentially regular margarine that has been expanded in volume by a type of chemical bonding with water. So sometimes I simply use a smaller amount of regular margarine and add water.

Applesauce:

This is one of my favorite replacements for fat. It adds moisture to baked goods without the unpleasant taste (and aftertaste) of other fat alternatives such as prune puree. Chocolate and applesauce still tastes like chocolate, but prune puree and chocolate tastes like prunes.

Corn Syrup:

This is another of my favorite fat replacements. In small amounts it helps baked goods retain moisture and increases their shelf life. Too much of it, however, can make them sticky. To avoid the sticky texture, I generally use it in conjunction with another moisturizing agent such as applesauce.

Egg Whites:

All of my recipes call for egg whites. I rarely use whole eggs, although a few recipes require one for taste and texture. But in most cases, egg whites work well as a replacement for whole eggs. In general it takes the whites of two large eggs to replace one whole egg. Be careful not to use too many egg whites because in excessive quantities they can make batter taste dry.

Taste Enhancers That Allow You to Cut Overall Fat

Cocoa:

Cocoa is a terrific flavoring agent for low-fat desserts. It is the most powerful source of pure chocolate flavor, with the least amount of fat, available for baking. It has less than one gram of fat per tablespoon and is free of cholesterol and sodium.

I strongly recommend that you use Dutch cocoa. It is darker than American-processed cocoa and has a much richer flavor. The European process, unlike the American process, uses alkali to neutralize the natural acidity of the cocoa powder. Not all markets carry Dutch cocoa, but it is well worth the extra effort to locate it. And cocoa is easy to use. You just blend it with the other dry ingredients rather than having to premelt it as is the case with other forms of chocolate.

Nuts:

Nuts taste wonderful in baked goods and add greatly to the texture, but they are all laden with fat. If I use them I do so in very small amounts. Instead, I prefer oats, Grape-Nuts, and Rice Krispies. These add the proper texture and, mixed with extracts, can supply much of the desired taste.

Extracts:

In general I use imitation vanilla extract rather than pure vanilla extract. I know this conflicts with most of the things you read in other cookbooks, but I find that pure vanilla extract can become bitter when used in too great a quantity, while imitation vanilla extract is extremely forgiving. And since vanilla has such a delicate taste, I like to use as much extract as I can to enhance the flavor.

You have to be very careful with almond or coconut extracts. These are very powerful and an extra half teaspoonful will ruin most recipes. They are, however, great sources of pure and potent flavor, so they can be very useful in low-fat recipes where flavor is at a premium.

Dairy:

Buttermilk contains no butter. It is milk that has had bacterial culture added to give it a slightly acidic taste and to thicken it. If you buy the low-fat style, it contains about the same amount of fat as low-fat milk: three to five grams per cup. I use it mostly in muffins and cakes because I find it enhances flavor and texture.

Fat-Free Sweetened Condensed Milk:

I was thrilled when I found this new product. I have always used sweetened condensed milk liberally in brownies and in many cheesecakes because it provides such a rich, milky taste. Having it available now in nonfat form allows me to reap the benefits of its wonderful baking properties in my low-fat recipes.

Sour Cream:

There are terrific fat-reduced sour cream substitutes. I love both light sour cream and fat-free sour cream in desserts. However, pay attention to where you use them. Fat-free sour cream is best only when the dessert is not baked or baked perfunctorily. For a dessert that requires any substantial amount of baking, I use light sour cream.

Cream Cheese:

Many recipes call for cream cheese. I would love to use light cream cheese all the time because it tastes great, but the fat content of most recipes is usually still too high if I do. So I dilute light cream cheese by mixing in fat-free cream cheese. If minimizing fat were my only consideration, I would use only fat-free cream cheese, but this is one fat-free product that just doesn't work. Any similarity between the taste of fat-free cream cheese and any other form of cream cheese is purely coincidental (and nonexistent). Mixing the cream cheeses in the proportions I recommend is the best compromise I could come up with between taste and fat content.

Cool Whip:

There is regular Cool Whip, light Cool Whip, and fat-free Cool Whip. I use them in recipes that call for whipped cream. Two tablespoons of regular Cool Whip contain 25 calories and 1.5 grams of fat; two tablespoons of light Cool Whip contain 20 calories and 1 gram of fat; and two tablespoons of fat-free Cool Whip contain 15 calories and no fat. They all seem to work well as a whipped cream replacement. Which one you choose depends upon how rich you want the dessert to taste, but unlike fat-free cream cheese, unadulterated fat-free Cool Whip usually tastes quite good by itself.

Supplies

Parchment Paper:

Lining the bottom of your cookie sheet with parchment paper will improve the quality of any cookie you bake. It stops the cookies from getting too brown on the bottom. It eases your cleanup and stops the cookies from sticking to the pan. Its only drawback is that it's somewhat difficult to find, so you might have to go to a baking specialty shop.

Corn Oil Spray:

I use corn oil spray to coat pans when I am not using parchment paper. Of course, it does contain fat, but the layer on the pan is so thin that it has virtually no effect on overall fat content. And it does not alter the taste of the dessert as would olive oil spray.

Ingredients

5

Muffins, Sticky Buns, Cinnamon Rolls, and More

If you're accustomed to the dry and tasteless quality of most fat-free muffins, you will be amazed at how delicious these are. I substitute applesauce for the oil, which normally provides moisture for muffins. This makes the muffin moist without leaving the unpleasant aftertaste that accompanies most concentrated-fruit fat substitutes. I use egg whites instead of whole eggs because the cholesterol-laden yolks don't contribute much to the taste or texture.

I also take special care to add generous amounts of powerful flavorings like vanilla extract, cinnamon, and lemon rind to make up for the taste loss that occurs with reduced fat. My final trick is to add puddings, which are virtually fat-free, to make the muffins rich-tasting yet light.

I divide my muffins into two basic categories: breakfast or bran-type muffins and dessert muffins. The bran-type are heavy, dense, and contain nutritious ingredients like oats, bran, whole wheat, and wheat germ. They are not as sweet as dessert muffins but are great for a somewhat sweet, nutritious, and convenient breakfast on the run. They also provide a healthy snack in the late afternoon when you may be running low on energy and need a pick-me-up.

Dessert muffins are light, cakelike, and sweet. They come in flavors like chocolate, orange, pistachio, and apple pie, and, of course, they are excellent for dessert. In fact dessert muffins are very much like little unfrosted cakes.

Bran Muffins

This is a rich and hearty bran muffin with a smooth texture that is not as gritty as that of a regular store-bought bran muffin. The chopped dates add a touch of welcome sweetness to counter the somewhat harsh flavor of the bran.

1/2 cup boiling water	1 teaspoon vanilla extract
1 cup 100% bran cereal	2 cups bran buds cereal
1 cup sugar	3 cups flour
1/4 cup Smart Beat margarine	2 1/2 teaspoons baking soda
1 tablespoon molasses	1 teaspoon salt
4 egg whites	1 teaspoon cinnamon
2 cups buttermilk	1/2 cup chopped dates

1. Preheat the oven to 350°F. Coat a muffin tin with nonstick spray and set aside.

2. In a small bowl pour the boiling water over the 100% bran cereal and set aside to cool.

3. In a large bowl cream the sugar, margarine, and molasses. Add the egg whites and mix well. Stir in the buttermilk and vanilla extract. Add the soaked 100% bran cereal and the bran buds cereal and mix well. Mix in the flour, baking soda, salt, cinnamon, and dates.

4. Spoon the batter into the prepared muffin tin so that the cup is ¾ full. Bake for 20 to 25 minutes or until a toothpick inserted into a muffin comes out clean. Cool for 5 minutes and remove the warm muffins from the pan.

Makes 24 muffins

One muffin contains: 141 calories, .9g of fat

Strawberry-Bran Muffins

This is one of my favorite hearty breakfast muffins. You could also use blueberries and blueberry preserves or raspberries and raspberry preserves or even fresh diced apples. They all taste great blended with cinnamon and bran.

1 3/4 cups All-Bran cereal

1 1/2 cups buttermilk

1 cup plus 1 tablespoon unsweetened applesauce

2 teaspoons canola oil

4 egg whites

1 cup sugar

1/2 cup light brown sugar

2 cups flour

1/2 cup whole wheat flour

1/4 cup bran

1 teaspoon baking powder

1 teaspoon baking soda

1 teaspoon cinnamon

1/4 teaspoon salt

3/4 cup chopped fresh or frozen unsweetened strawberries

1/4 cup plus 1 tablespoon light strawberry preserves

1. Preheat the oven to 400°F. Coat a muffin tin with nonstick spray and set aside.

2. In a large bowl combine the All-Bran and buttermilk and let stand for 5 minutes or until the cereal is softened. Add the applesauce, oil, and egg whites and blend until smooth. Beat in the sugars and mix until smooth. Stir in the flours, bran, baking powder, baking soda, cinnamon, and salt and mix well.

4. Fill the prepared muffin cups ⅓ full. Place 1 teaspoon of the chopped strawberries on the batter. Pour the remaining batter on top of the strawberries until the muffin cups are ¾ full. Spoon 1 teaspoon of chopped strawberries and 1 teaspoon of strawberry preserves on top of each muffin.

5. Bake for 20 to 25 minutes or until a toothpick inserted into a muffin comes out clean. Cool for 5 minutes and remove from the tin.

Makes 16 muffins

One muffin contains: 210 calories, 2.6g of fat

Pumpkin Pie Oat-Bran Muffins

Oat bran is high in fiber and lowers serum cholesterol (according to some but not all research), but it has a harsh and bitter taste. It took me dozens of failed attempts before I was able to come up with oat-bran muffins of my own that really tasted good. It was one of my most difficult challenges.

This particular muffin has the characteristic golden color of pumpkin and exudes the flavor of traditional pumpkin pie spice and cinnamon. The strong flavors of the spices keep the muffin from being overpowered by the flavor of the oat bran.

3 egg whites

1/2 cup buttermilk

3 tablespoons canola oil

1 1/2 cups canned pumpkin

1/4 cup unsweetened applesauce

1 3/4 cups sugar

1 tablespoon vanilla extract

1/2 cup whole wheat flour

1 1/2 cups oat bran

1 1/4 cups rolled oats

1/4 cup wheat germ

1 tablespoon baking powder

2 tablespoons pumpkin pie spice

1 teaspoon salt

1 cup raisins

1. Preheat the oven to 350°F. Coat a muffin tin with nonstick spray and set aside.

2. In a large bowl mix together the egg whites, buttermilk, and oil. Add the pumpkin, applesauce, sugar, and vanilla extract and mix well.

3. Stir in the flour, oat bran, rolled oats, wheat germ, baking powder, pumpkin pie spice, and salt. Beat until smooth. Fold in the raisins.

4. Fill each muffin cup to the very top. (They don't rise much.) Bake for 50 to 60 minutes or until a toothpick inserted into a muffin comes out clean. Cool for 5 minutes and remove from the muffin tin.

Makes 14 muffins

One muffin contains: 255 calories, 4.6g of fat

Apple Oat-Bran Muffins

A substantial and satisfying breakfast, apple oat-bran muffins are highly nutritious and supply the energy necessary to jump-start your day. If you are normally pressed for time in the mornings you can freeze a batch of these and thaw them in the microwave as needed so that you will always have on hand a well-balanced, extremely healthy breakfast for a family member on the go. And for a change you won't have to fight with your children to get them to eat nutritiously. The combination of honey, cinnamon, and fresh apples is delicious.

3 egg whites

1/2 cup buttermilk

1 3/8 cups honey

3 tablespoons canola oil

3/4 cup unsweetened applesauce

1 tablespoon vanilla extract

1/2 cup whole wheat flour

1 1/2 cups oat bran

1 1/4 cups rolled oats

1/4 cup wheat germ

2 tablespoons cinnamon

1 tablespoon baking powder

2 cups finely diced, unpeeled green apples

1. Preheat the oven to 350°F. Coat a muffin tin with nonstick spray and set aside.

2. In a large bowl mix together the egg whites, buttermilk, honey, oil, applesauce, and vanilla extract. Add the flour, oat bran, rolled oats, wheat germ, cinnamon, and baking powder and mix until smooth. Fold in the apples.

3. Fill each muffin cup to the very top. Bake for 50 to 60 minutes or until a toothpick inserted into a muffin comes out clean. Cool for 5 minutes and remove from the muffin tin.

Makes 14 muffins

One muffin contains: 223 calories, 4.5g of fat

Banana Oat-Bran Muffins

This muffin is heavy, hearty, and somewhat sweet. If you like sweets at breakfast, this muffin and a cup of coffee or a glass of milk will make a completely satisfying meal. And these are the most powerful and nutrition-packed muffins I know of. Look at the basic ingredients: oat bran, oats, wheat germ, whole wheat flour, Grape-Nuts, egg whites, bananas, and applesauce. I feel healthier just reading the list.

3 medium, very ripe bananas, mashed

3 egg whites

1 cup unsweetened applesauce

1 3/4 cups sugar

3 tablespoons canola oil

1/2 cup buttermilk

1 tablespoon vanilla extract

1 1/2 cups oat bran

1 cup rolled oats

1/2 cup whole wheat flour

1 tablespoon baking powder

1 teaspoon salt

1/2 cup Grape-Nuts

1. Preheat the oven to 350°F. Coat a muffin tin with nonstick spray and set aside.

2. In a large bowl combine the bananas, egg whites, and applesauce and mix until blended. Stir in the sugar, oil, buttermilk, and vanilla extract and mix until smooth. Blend in the oat bran, oats, flour, baking powder, salt, and Grape-Nuts.

3. Fill the muffin cups to the top. These muffins hardly rise. Bake for 50 to 55 minutes or until a toothpick inserted into a muffin comes out clean.

Makes 15 muffins

One muffin contains: 220 calories, 4.0g of fat

Pumpkin Muffins

This is one of the moistest muffins I have ever made. Pumpkins have a surprisingly benevolent effect on baked goods. Not only do they color the muffin a golden bronze, but they also add a tremendous amount of moisture while supplying a distinctive vegetable flavor that blends beautifully with cinnamon. Great as a dessert anytime, this muffin will make a fitting contribution to your Thanksgiving meal.

6 egg whites	2 teaspoons baking powder
2 cups sugar	1 teaspoon baking soda
2/3 cup unsweetened applesauce	1 teaspoon salt
1 tablespoon canola oil	2 teaspoons cinnamon
2 cups canned pumpkin	1 teaspoon pumpkin pie spice
2 cups flour	

1. Preheat the oven to 350°F. Coat a muffin tin with nonstick spray and set aside.

2. In a large bowl beat the egg whites until foamy. Add the sugar, applesauce, oil, and pumpkin and blend until smooth. Stir in the flour, baking powder, baking soda, salt, cinnamon, and pumpkin pie spice. Beat until smooth.

3. Fill the muffin cups ¾ full. Bake for 35 to 45 minutes or until a toothpick inserted into the center of a muffin comes out clean. Cool for 5 minutes and remove from the muffin tin.

Makes 16 muffins

One muffin contains: 182 calories, 1.1g of fat

Applesauce Spice Muffins

These make excellent breakfast muffins. They are dense, hearty, and nutritious, loaded with apples and applesauce. This is an in-between muffin, sweeter than a typical oat-bran or bran muffin but not nearly as sweet as a dessert muffin.

2 cups plus 2 tablespoons flour

1 3/4 cups sugar

1 teaspoon baking powder

1 teaspoon baking soda

1 teaspoon salt

2 teaspoons cinnamon

1 1/3 cups unsweetened applesauce

1/3 cup Smart Beat margarine, melted

4 egg whites

1 teaspoon vanilla extract

1 cup (1 medium) chopped peeled apple

1/4 cup Grape-Nuts

Topping:

2 tablespoons sugar

1 teaspoon cinnamon

1. Preheat the oven to 350°F. Coat a muffin tin with nonstick spray and set aside.

2. In a large bowl combine the flour, sugar, baking powder, baking soda, salt, and cinnamon and blend well. Add the applesauce, margarine, egg whites, and vanilla extract and blend at low speed until moistened.

3. Beat at high speed for 2 minutes or until smooth. Stir in the apple and Grape-Nuts. Spoon the batter into muffin cups, filling each to the top.

4. To make topping: In a small bowl mix the sugar and cinnamon. Sprinkle the topping evenly over each muffin.

5. Bake for 30 to 40 minutes or until a toothpick inserted into a muffin comes out clean. Cool and remove from the muffin tin.

Makes 12 muffins

One muffin contains: 243 calories, 1.2g of fat

Wholesome Oatmeal Muffins

This muffin is much lighter than a bran or an oat-bran muffin, but still provides some of the nutritional benefits of the heavier muffins. I use fruit preserves in the muffin, and my favorite is light boysenberry with seeds, but this recipe works equally well with strawberry or raspberry. I would not suggest using jelly because it becomes runny during the baking process. The preserves bake into the muffin and provide moisture, a deep plum color, and a sweet fruit flavor. Since the batter itself is not very sweet, the preserves are an intrinsic part of the muffin.

1 1/2 cups rolled oats	1 1/2 cups flour
1 1/4 cups boiling water	1 teaspoon baking soda
5 egg whites	1 teaspoon baking powder
1/2 cup unsweetened applesauce	1/2 teaspoon salt
2 teaspoons vanilla extract	1 1/2 teaspoons cinnamon
1 cup sugar	1/2 cup Grape-Nuts
1/2 cup dark brown sugar, packed	5 tablespoons light boysenberry preserves
1/2 cup light brown sugar, packed	

1. Preheat the oven to 350°F. Coat a muffin tin with nonstick spray and set aside.

2. In a small bowl combine the oats and boiling water and set aside to cool.

3. In a large bowl add together the egg whites, applesauce, and vanilla extract and mix until smooth. Add the sugars and mix until well blended. Stir in the flour, baking soda, baking powder, salt, cinnamon, and Grape-Nuts. Mix well.

4. Spoon the batter into the muffin tin so that the cups are ¾ full. Place 1 teaspoon of light preserves on top of each muffin. Bake for 40 to 45 minutes or until a toothpick inserted into a muffin comes out clean.

Makes 14 muffins

One muffin contains: 227 calories, .7g of fat

Apple Pie Muffins

This scrumptious muffin is supermoist and bursting with all the flavor of an apple pie, yet it has the texture of a muffin. Do not let the incongruity of this description dissuade you from making it. It is one of my no-miss, sure-thing winners.

4 egg whites

1/4 cup nonfat milk

1/4 cup buttermilk

1/2 cup unsweetened applesauce

2 teaspoons vanilla extract

2 cups sugar

2 cups flour

1 tablespoon baking powder

1 tablespoon cinnamon

1 teaspoon salt

1 package (3.4 ounces) instant vanilla pudding mix

1 cup apple pie filling

Topping:

6 tablespoons sugar

1 tablespoon cinnamon

1. Preheat the oven to 350°F. Coat a muffin tin with nonstick spray, fill with muffin papers, and set aside.

2. In a large bowl mix together the egg whites, nonfat milk, buttermilk, applesauce, and vanilla extract. Add the sugar and beat until smooth. Stir in the flour, baking powder, cinnamon, salt, and pudding mix, and beat until smooth.

3. Fold in the apple pie filling and mix until smooth. Pour into the prepared muffin tin, filling each cup ¾ full.

4. To make topping: In a small bowl mix the sugar and cinnamon. Sprinkle 1 teaspoon of topping mixture on each muffin.

5. Bake for 35 to 40 minutes or until a toothpick inserted into a muffin comes out clean.

Makes 15 muffins

One muffin contains: 219 calories, .4g of fat

Blueberry Muffins

There is a trick to making these muffins taste and look great: Drop the blueberries into each muffin by hand. If you add the blueberries all at once, the color runs, and you get an unappetizing bluish muffin with little distinction between the blueberry and the batter. My fat-free muffin will satisfy your morning sweet tooth without the 300 to 500 calories and the 20 grams or more of fat contained in most regular blueberry muffins. If you use frozen berries, do not thaw them because the color runs and the whole muffin turns blue. For variety you can use other fruits, such as cranberries or raspberries.

4 egg whites

2 teaspoons vanilla extract

1 cup buttermilk

1/2 cup unsweetened applesauce

2 cups sugar

2 cups flour

1 package (3.4 ounces) instant vanilla pudding mix

1 tablespoon baking powder

1 teaspoon salt

1 cup fresh or frozen blueberries

1. Preheat the oven to 350°F. Coat the muffin tin with nonstick spray and line with muffin papers.

2. In a large bowl add the egg whites, vanilla extract, buttermilk, and applesauce and combine with a hand mixer. Add the sugar and blend well. Add the flour, vanilla pudding mix, baking powder, and salt and mix well.

3. Spoon the batter into the muffin cups, filling each half full. Add 4 to 5 blueberries to each muffin. Fill the rest of the muffin cups with batter. Add 4 to 5 more blueberries to the top of each muffin.

4. Bake for 35 to 40 minutes or until a toothpick inserted into the muffin comes out clean.

Makes 12 muffins

One muffin contains: 242 calories, .7g of fat

Fresh Lemon Muffins with Lemon Drizzle

Lemon has the sharp, distinctive, and authoritative taste that makes it a particularly attractive fruit in low-fat baked goods, where flavor is at a premium. You will love it in this muffin because the sugary drizzled glaze perfectly balances the tartness of the lemon.

2 cups flour

1 tablespoon baking powder

1 teaspoon salt

4 egg whites

3/4 cup low-fat buttermilk

1/4 cup lemon juice

1/2 cup unsweetened applesauce

2 cups sugar

1 teaspoon grated lemon zest

1 teaspoon vanilla extract

1 package (3.4 ounces) instant lemon pudding mix

Lemon Drizzle:

2 cups powdered sugar

2 tablespoons lemon juice

1 tablespoon corn syrup

1. Preheat the oven to 350°F. Coat a muffin tin with nonstick spray and line with muffin papers.

2. In a small bowl sift together the flour, baking powder, and salt and set aside. In a large bowl combine the egg whites, buttermilk, lemon juice, and applesauce and mix until smooth. Stir in the sugar, lemon zest, and vanilla extract and mix well. Add the flour mixture and pudding mix and beat until smooth.

3. Pour the batter into the prepared muffin tin. Bake for 40 to 45 minutes or until a toothpick inserted into the center of a muffin comes out clean.

4. To make drizzle: In a small bowl combine the powdered sugar, lemon juice, and corn syrup and blend until smooth. Drizzle over the tops of the muffins.

Makes 14 muffins

One muffin contains: 288 calories, .4g of fat

Poppy Seed Muffins

This is a light dessert muffin, not as sweet as the fruit muffins. The poppy seeds blended throughout impart a distinctive nutty flavor and a crunchy texture to the mellow vanilla aroma of the batter. If you're a fan of muffin tops, try this one dusted with a little powdered sugar. It's one of the best.

1 package (18.25 ounces) Duncan Hines Butter Recipe cake mix

2/3 cup water

1/4 cup Smart Beat margarine

1/4 cup unsweetened applesauce

4 egg whites

1 teaspoon vanilla extract

2 tablespoons plus 1 teaspoon poppy seeds

2 tablespoons powdered sugar for topping

1. Preheat the oven to 350°F. Coat a muffin tin with nonstick spray and line with muffin papers. Set aside.

2. In a large bowl combine the cake mix, water, margarine, applesauce, egg whites, vanilla extract, and poppy seeds and mix until blended. Beat on high speed until blended.

3. Pour the batter into the prepared muffin tin so that each muffin paper is filled to the top. Bake for 20 to 25 minutes or until a toothpick inserted into a muffin comes out clean.

4. Allow muffins to cool and dust with the powdered sugar.

Makes 12 muffins

One muffin contains: 208 calories, 5.4g of fat

Pistachio Muffins

Most people aren't initially impressed with the idea of a pistachio-flavored muffin. They have difficulty imagining what it tastes like. But they are pleasantly surprised when they try this muffin, and it has become one of our restaurant's most popular items.

In baked goods or ice cream the flavor commonly considered to be pistachio is really almond. Green-tinted batter adds to the pistachio perception.

4 egg whites

1 cup buttermilk

1/2 cup plus 2 tablespoons unsweetened applesauce

1 teaspoon almond extract

4 drops green food coloring

2 cups sugar

2 cups flour

1 package (3.4 ounces) instant pistachio pudding mix

1 tablespoon baking powder

1 teaspoon salt

2 tablespoons powdered sugar for topping

1. Preheat the oven to 350°F. Coat a muffin tin with nonstick spray, line with muffin papers, and set aside.

2. In a large bowl combine the egg whites, buttermilk, applesauce, almond extract, and food coloring and mix until smooth. Stir in the sugar and blend well. Mix in the flour, pudding mix, baking powder, and salt and beat until smooth.

3. Fill the muffin papers ¾ full. Bake for 35 to 45 minutes or until a toothpick inserted into a muffin comes out clean.

4. Cool for 5 minutes and remove from pan. Sprinkle powdered sugar on top of each muffin before serving.

Makes 14 muffins

One muffin contains: 204 calories, .5g of fat

Peach Pie Muffins

This is a light, sweet, fruity dessert muffin. Bottled peach nectar and canned peach filling give it that peach pie taste. And you can enjoy it year-round because you don't have to wait for fresh peaches to come in season.

4 egg whites

1/2 cup peach nectar

1/2 cup plus 2 tablespoons unsweetened applesauce

2 teaspoons vanilla extract

2 cups sugar

2 cups flour

1 package (3.4 ounces) instant vanilla pudding mix

1 teaspoon salt

1 tablespoon baking powder

10.5 ounces (1/2 can) peach pie filling

1. Preheat the oven to 350°F. Coat a muffin tin with nonstick spray, line with muffin papers, and set aside.

2. In a large bowl combine the egg whites, peach nectar, applesauce, and vanilla extract. Add the sugar and blend well. Mix in the flour, pudding mix, salt, and baking powder and beat until smooth. Fold in the peach pie filling.

3. Fill the muffin papers ¾ full. Bake for 35 to 45 minutes or until a toothpick inserted into a muffin comes out clean. Cool for 5 minutes and remove from the tin.

Makes 14 muffins

One muffin contains: 228 calories, .4g of fat

Chocolate Muffins

For those of us who require a chocolate version of every kind of baked good, this pure chocolate muffin gets the prize in the muffin category. Not only is it exceptionally moist, an abundance of high-quality Dutch cocoa produces a deep, rich color and a formidable chocolate flavor. With a dusting of powdered sugar and a sprinkling of minichocolate chips, you can't help reaching for one of these dark jewels.

1 cup low-fat chocolate milk

1/3 cup unsweetened applesauce

4 egg whites

2 teaspoons vanilla extract

2 cups sugar

2 cups flour

1/2 cup unsweetened Dutch cocoa

1 package (3.4 ounces) instant chocolate pudding mix

1 tablespoon baking powder

1 teaspoon salt

1 tablespoon minichocolate chips

5 tablespoons powdered sugar for topping

1. Preheat the oven to 350°F. Coat a muffin tin with nonstick spray, line with muffin papers, and set aside.

2. In a large bowl mix together the chocolate milk, applesauce, egg whites, and vanilla extract. Add the sugar, flour, cocoa, pudding mix, baking powder, and salt and beat until smooth.

3. Pour into the prepared muffin tin until each cup is ¾ full. Sprinkle 4 or 5 minichocolate chips on each muffin.

4. Bake for 35 to 40 minutes or until a toothpick inserted into a muffin comes out clean. Cool for 5 minutes. Remove from the tin.

5. Cool completely and dust with the powdered sugar before serving.

Makes 14 muffins

One muffin contains: 240 calories, 1.1g of fat

Orange Muffins

Orange lovers will rejoice at this light, bracing, fat-free dessert muffin. The sweet citrus tang of orange juice and orange zest create a clean and refreshing taste.

1 cup orange juice

1/2 cup plus 2 tablespoons unsweetened applesauce

4 egg whites

1 tablespoon orange extract

2 cups sugar

2 cups flour

1 tablespoon baking powder

1 teaspoon salt

1 1/4 teaspoons grated orange zest

1. Preheat the oven to 350°F. Coat a muffin tin with nonstick spray, line with muffin papers, and set aside.

2. In a large bowl combine the orange juice, applesauce, egg whites, and orange extract and mix until blended. Stir in the sugar and mix until smooth. Add the flour, baking powder, salt, and orange zest and beat until smooth.

3. Spoon the batter into the muffin papers, filling each ¾ full. Bake for 35 to 45 minutes or until a toothpick inserted into a muffin comes out clean.

Makes 14 muffins

One muffin contains: 195 calories, .2g of fat

Strawberry Jell-O Muffins

This bright pink muffin is definitely for kids, or for grown-up kids who still like the flavor of strawberry Jell-O. But unlike most kids' desserts it is virtually fat-free.

2 cups flour

1 tablespoon baking powder

1 teaspoon salt

2 cups sugar

4 egg whites

1 cup water

1/2 cup unsweetened applesauce

2 teaspoons vanilla extract

1 package (3.25 ounces) strawberry-flavored Jell-O mix

5 tablespoons sugar

1. Preheat the oven to 350°F. Coat a muffin tin with nonstick spray, line with muffin papers, and set aside.

2. In a large bowl combine the flour, baking powder, and salt. Mix in the sugar, egg whites, and water. Add the applesauce and vanilla extract and mix well. Stir in the Jell-O and mix until smooth.

3. Pour the batter into the prepared muffin tin, filling each cup almost to the top. Sprinkle 1 teaspoon of sugar over the top of each muffin. Bake for 40 to 45 minutes or until a toothpick inserted into a muffin comes out clean.

Makes 14 muffins

One muffin contains: 225 calories, .2g of fat

Caramel Sticky Buns

The only thing that equals the terrific flavor of these glistening, gooey, golden lit-tle rolls is their looks. They are adorable, like baby cinnamon buns. Chewy rather than doughy, they are heavier than cinnamon rolls and not quite as sweet. They are best served piping hot out of the oven as the aroma of cinnamon pervades the house.

Topping:

1/4 cup Smart Beat margarine

1/4 cup dark brown sugar, packed

2 tablespoons light corn syrup

1/4 cup rolled oats

Coating:

5 teaspoons sugar

1 teaspoon cinnamon

Buns:

1 can (7.5 ounces) refrigerated buttermilk biscuits

1. Preheat the oven to 375°F. Coat a muffin tin with nonstick spray and set aside.

2. To make topping: In a small bowl combine the margarine, brown sugar, corn syrup, and oats. Place a tablespoonful of topping in each muffin cup.

3. To make coating: In a medium bowl combine the sugar and cinnamon and set aside.

4. Separate the dough into 10 biscuits. Cut each biscuit into 6 pieces, yielding 60 pieces. Toss the pieces in the prepared coating mixture.

5. Place 5 pieces of coated biscuit dough in each muffin cup. Place the muffin tin on a cookie sheet to guard against spills. Bake for 15 minutes or until golden. Cool for one minute in the pan and then invert onto waxed paper.

Makes 12 sticky buns

One bun contains: 92 calories, 1.4g of fat

Mini-Cinnamon Rolls

In most cinnamon rolls the fat resides in the butter-soaked dough. In its stead, strange as it may seem, I use a refrigerated pizza crust and a small amount of Smart Beat margarine. This combination is very low in fat but tastes great. Since the rest of the ingredients are standard you will still get that warm and familiar aroma of sweet cinnamon and fresh-baked pastry.

These rolls are considerably smaller than the usual enormous ones. Those big rolls used to put me a quandary—I didn't want to leave so much good food on my plate, so I continued eating even though I wished I were already done. These minirolls allow perfect portion control.

Rolls:

1 can (10 ounces) refrigerated pizza dough (I prefer Pillsbury.)

3 tablespoons Smart Beat margarine

5 tablespoons sugar

1 tablespoon cinnamon

Glaze:

5 tablespoons powdered sugar

1 1/2 to 2 teaspoons nonfat milk

1. Preheat the oven to 425°F. Line a baking sheet or cookie sheet with parchment paper or waxed paper.

2. Open the can of pizza dough and roll it out flat on the baking sheet. With a pastry brush spread 1½ tablespoons of the margarine over the entire top of the pizza dough.

3. Combine the sugar and cinnamon and sprinkle 2 tablespoons of this mixture over the top of the pizza dough, covering the spread margarine. Starting at the shorter side, roll up the pizza dough so that the sugar, cinnamon, and margarine are now layered inside of it.

4. Spread the remaining 1½ tablespoons of margarine over the outside of the rolled dough. Sprinkle 2 tablespoons of the remaining sugar and cinnamon over the outside of the rolled dough.

5. With a sharp knife cut the roll crosswise into 16 slices. To do this you first cut the roll in half, then cut each half in half again, and repeat until you have 16 slices.

6. Place the dough slices on the baking sheet. Sprinkle the remaining sugar and cinnamon mixture over the top of each sliced cinnamon roll. Bake for 8 minutes. Remove from the oven and cool.

7. To make glaze: In a small bowl blend the sugar and enough milk for the desired glaze consistency. Drizzle the mixture over the cooled rolls.

Makes 16 rolls

One roll contains: 80 calories, 1.0g of fat

Peanut Butter and Jelly Sweet Rolls

This is a great snack for the kids when they come home from school. It is like a sweet peanut butter and jelly sandwich, and the kids will want to drink plenty of cold nonfat milk to wash it down. It looks gooey and tempting, with colorful jam and white sugary glaze adorning the top. Eat them fresh from the oven—they don't keep well. (The high-fat version of this recipe contains 250 calories and 12 grams of fat.)

Rolls:

1 can (7.5 ounces) refrigerated buttermilk biscuits

10 teaspoons reduced-fat peanut butter

5 teaspoons light preserves (I like Knotts boysenberry.)

Glaze:

1/4 cup powdered sugar

1 to 2 teaspoons nonfat milk

1. Preheat the oven to 450°F. Coat an 8-inch square or 9-inch round pan with non-stick spray.

2. Separate the dough into 10 biscuits. Cut each biscuit into two layers so that you can make a sandwich. Spoon one teaspoon of peanut butter onto the center of one of the halves. Put the other half on top of this. Pinch the edges to seal in the peanut butter.

3. Place the biscuits in the pan so they are not touching. With your thumb, make an imprint in the center of each roll. Fill the imprint with ½ teaspoon of preserves.

4. Bake for 8 to 10 minutes or until golden brown. Remove from the oven and allow to cool slightly.

5. To make glaze: In a small bowl blend the sugar and enough milk to obtain the desired consistency. Drizzle over the still warm rolls. Serve immediately.

Makes 10 rolls

One roll contains: 105 calories, 2.5g of fat

Amaretto Cheese Danish

A rich amaretto glaze covers this grown-up miniature sweet roll. It has a rich and smooth texture, thanks to the cream cheese baked into the batter.

Danish:

3 ounces low-fat cream cheese

1/2 teaspoon almond extract

1/4 cup powdered sugar

1 tablespoon chopped almonds

1 can (10 ounces) refrigerated pizza dough

1 egg white

1/2 teaspoon water

Glaze:

1/2 cup powdered sugar

1/4 teaspoon almond extract

2 teaspoons nonfat milk

1. Preheat the oven to 425°F. Coat a cookie sheet with nonstick spray and set aside.

2. To make danish: In a small bowl beat the cream cheese, almond extract, and powdered sugar until smooth. Stir in the chopped almonds and set aside.

3. Open the can of dough and roll the dough into a rectangle. Spread the cream cheese mixture over the dough to within ¼ inch of the edges.

4. Start at one end and roll up the rectangle, firmly pinching the edges and ends to seal. Slice the roll crosswise into 20 small cylindrical pieces. Place them on the prepared cookie sheet.

5. In a small bowl combine the egg white and water and brush over the rolls. Bake for 12 minutes or until golden brown.

6. To make glaze: In a small bowl blend the powdered sugar, almond extract, and milk until smooth. Drizzle ½ teaspoon over each warm roll. Serve warm.

Makes 20 rolls

One roll contains: 66 calories, 1.4g of fat

Cinnamon-Marshmallow Puffs

This is a lovely surprise dessert. A marshmallow in the center of each puff's buttery dough melts and disappears during the baking process, leaving the center hollow. It seeps into the dough and mixes with the light margarine to produce a rich, juicy, cinnamon-soaked puff. The texture is similar to that of a donut, with a dominant cinnamon flavor and a gooey, candied bottom.

Puffs:

1/4 cup sugar

1 teaspoon cinnamon

1 can (7.5 ounces) refrigerated
  buttermilk biscuits

10 marshmallows

3 tablespoons Smart Beat
  margarine, melted

Glaze:

1/4 cup powdered sugar

1/2 teaspoon vanilla extract

1 1/2 teaspoons nonfat or low-fat milk

1. Preheat the oven to 375°F. In a small bowl combine the sugar and cinnamon and set aside.

2. Separate the dough into 10 biscuits and cut each in half. Flatten each half slightly.

3. Dip a marshmallow in melted margarine and roll in the prepared sugar/cinnamon mixture. Place the marshmallow on a flattened biscuit half. Place the other half of the biscuit on the marshmallow. Firmly pinch the edges of the biscuit to completely cover and seal the marshmallow.

4. Dip the sealed biscuit in the remaining margarine and sprinkle with the remaining sugar/cinnamon mixture. Place in the muffin cup of an ungreased muffin tin. Repeat with the remaining marshmallows and biscuits.

5. Bake for 10 to 12 minutes or until light golden brown. Immediately remove from the muffin cups and cool on waxed paper.

6. To make glaze: In a small bowl mix together the powdered sugar, vanilla extract, and enough milk to reach drizzling consistency. Drizzle over the warm rolls.

Makes 10 puffs

One puff contains: 115 calories, 1.3g of fat

Donut Holes

These are fun treats for the kids, and just the name "Donut Holes" makes the kids want them. The coverings provide the basic flavors, and the small spheres of dough can be rolled in everything from cinnamon and sugar to sprinkles.

Donut Holes:

1 can (7.5 ounces) refrigerated buttermilk biscuits

2 tablespoons Smart Beat margarine, melted

Topping:

2 tablespoons sugar

1 1/2 teaspoons cinnamon

Glaze:

1 cup powdered sugar

1 tablespoon Smart Beat margarine

1/2 teaspoon vanilla extract

1 to 2 tablespoons nonfat milk

1. Preheat the oven to 450°F. Line a cookie sheet with parchment paper or coat with nonstick spray and set aside.

2. To make donut holes: Open the can of biscuits and separate them into 10 biscuits. Cut each biscuit into 4 equal pieces. Roll each piece into a ball.

3. Dip the balls in the melted margarine. Roll the entire ball so it is well coated. Place on a cookie sheet. They don't spread much so they can be close together.

4. Bake for 6 to 7 minutes or until just beginning to become slightly brown. Remove from the oven to cool.

5. To make glaze: In a small bowl mix together the powdered sugar, margarine, vanilla extract, and milk. Blend until smooth. Dip each cooled donut into the glaze. To make topping: Combine the sugar and cinnamon in a small bowl. Roll some in the sugar/cinnamon mixture and leave some with only the glaze.

Makes 40 donut holes

One donut hole contains: 29 calories, .3g of fat

Raspberry Swirls

The dominant flavors in this little white and deep ruby roll are raspberry and sweet bread. In fact it tastes like a raspberry coffee cake and it makes an excellent companion for your morning coffee.

Rolls:

1 can (7.5 ounces) refrigerated buttermilk biscuits

Glaze:

1/2 cup powdered sugar

2 teaspoons low-fat milk

Topping:

2 tablespoons Smart Beat margarine, melted

1/4 cup plus 1 tablespoon light red raspberry preserves

1. Preheat the oven to 425°F. Coat a cookie sheet with nonstick spray and set aside.

2. Open the can of biscuits and cut each biscuit in half. Place them on the prepared cookie sheet. Carefully brush the rolls with half of the melted margarine.

3. Make a deep thumbprint in the center of each roll. Fill the thumbprint with 1 teaspoon of the preserves.

4. Bake for 8 minutes or until golden. Immediately remove from the pan. Brush a second time with the remaining melted margarine. Cool slightly.

5. To make glaze: In a small bowl blend the powdered sugar and milk until smooth. Drizzle the glaze over the warm rolls.

Makes 16 rolls

One roll contains: 57 calories, .7g of fat

Quick Breads

Quick breads use fast-acting leavening agents like baking soda or baking powder rather than slow-acting yeast. They are easy to make and very versatile. Not only can you enjoy them for a hearty and nutritious breakfast, but they make delectable accompaniments for soup, salad, chili, and even your Thanksgiving turkey dinner. Wrapped up in clear cellophane and tied with a decorative ribbon, they make the perfect hostess gift.

Quick breads store and freeze beautifully. You can bake extra quantities and, after they are cool, encase them in plastic wrap. In this state they will keep in the refrigerator for at least a week or in the freezer for several months. You will be glad you have them when an unexpected guest arrives. Just pop one in the microwave for about a minute, and you will have a warm quick bread that tastes as if it had just come from the oven.

Corn Bread

The aroma of hot corn bread is welcome on a cold evening, and a crunchy slice of toasted corn bread with honey butter can soften the morning's chill. Corn is low in fat and what's there is unsaturated. And despite its name, buttermilk is generally made from skim or low-fat milk and contains virtually no butter and little fat. Bacterial culture is added to the skim milk that is left when butter is churned from cream, and this gives the buttermilk its characteristic flavor, thickness, and acidity.

2 egg whites

1 cup buttermilk

1/4 cup Smart Beat margarine

1 cup yellow cornmeal

1 cup flour

1/3 cup sugar

1/2 teaspoon salt

1 tablespoon plus 1 teaspoon baking powder

1. Preheat the oven to 425°F. Coat an 8- or 8½-inch loaf pan with nonstick spray and set aside.

2. In a bowl combine the egg whites, buttermilk, and margarine and mix using your hand mixer until blended. Add the cornmeal, flour, sugar, salt, and baking powder one at a time and mix until blended.

3. Pour into the prepared loaf pan. Bake for 20 to 25 minutes until golden.

Makes 12 servings

One serving contains: 124 calories, 1.5g of fat

Zucchini Bread

I love the threads of green running through this golden brown bread. Because it is dense and hearty and not particularly sweet, it is not normally eaten for dessert. I like it for breakfast topped with a thin layer of light cream cheese along with a bowl of fresh fruit. My friends enjoy it when they come for lunch and I serve it in a basket of assorted breads to accompany a garden salad or chicken salad.

3 egg whites

2 teaspoons canola oil

3/4 cup plus 1 tablespoon unsweet- ened applesauce

1 teaspoon vanilla extract

1 1/8 cups flour

1 cup sugar

1 teaspoon baking soda

1 teaspoon cinnamon

1/4 teaspoon salt

1/2 teaspoon nutmeg

1/4 teaspoon cloves

1/4 teaspoon ginger

1 cup shredded zucchini (about 1 medium zucchini)

1/4 cup Grape-Nuts

1. Preheat the oven to 350°F. Coat an 8-inch loaf pan with nonstick spray and set aside.

2. In a food processor, combine the egg whites, oil, applesauce, and vanilla extract and mix well. Add the flour, sugar, baking soda, cinnamon, salt, nutmeg, cloves, and ginger and mix well. Add the zucchini and Grape-Nuts and mix until blended.

3. Pour into the prepared loaf pan. Bake for 1 hour or until a toothpick inserted into the center comes out clean.

Makes 12 servings

One serving contains: 132 calories, less than 1g of fat

Banana Bread

I am constantly looking for ways to keep low-fat cooking interesting, and using banana breads in unusual settings is one way to accomplish this. Our restaurant customers appreciate the way we serve banana bread as an accompaniment to a fresh fruit plate, and I enjoy it toasted at breakfast with an egg white omelette as a nice change from regular toast.

The key to an exceptional banana bread is to use overripe bananas. In fact, when the bananas on your counter start to develop that dark squashy look and no one wants to eat them anymore, forget about throwing them out. It's time to make banana bread. Overripe bananas are very sweet and flavorful and make the bread soft and moist.

This banana bread is particularly nutritious because not only are the bananas loaded with potassium, but the applesauce and Grape-Nuts are formidable sources of fiber.

3 very ripe bananas

1 cup sugar

2 egg whites

1/4 cup Smart Beat margarine, melted

1 1/2 cups flour

1 teaspoon baking soda

1 teaspoon salt

1 teaspoon vanilla extract

1/4 cup Grape-Nuts

1. Preheat the oven to 325°F. Coat an 8½-inch loaf pan with nonstick spray and set aside.

2. In a large bowl mash the bananas. Add the sugar and blend until smooth. Stir in the egg whites and margarine. Add the flour, baking soda, salt, and vanilla extract and beat until smooth. Fold in the Grape-Nuts.

3. Pour into the prepared pan. Bake for 65 to 75 minutes or until a toothpick inserted into the center comes out clean. Cool for 5 minutes and remove from the pan.

Makes 12 servings

One serving contains: 166 calories, 1.0g of fat

Date-Nut Bread

The fragrance of this bread, fresh from the oven, will attract your family to the kitchen, and you may have to fight them off to keep them from eating it all before the meal begins. It is an excellent addition to a simple menu of soup and salad, but I like it with breakfast. I know it says "date-nut," but there are no nuts, which are frighteningly high in fat. This bread gets its wonderful nutty flavor from Grape-Nuts, which is extremely low in fat. Applesauce provides moisture, and the powerful aroma and natural sweetness of the dates create the bread's distinctive taste. You may want to top it with a Cinnamon-Raisin Cream Cheese (page 163).

1 1/2 cups chopped dates

1 1/2 teaspoons baking soda

1 cup boiling water

4 egg whites

2 teaspoons vanilla extract

1 cup sugar

1/3 cup unsweetened applesauce

2 cups flour

1/2 cup Grape-Nuts

1. Preheat the oven to 350°F. Coat an 8-inch loaf pan with nonstick spray and set aside. Place the dates, baking soda, and boiling water in a small bowl and mix well. Let cool and set aside.

2. In another bowl combine the egg whites, vanilla extract, sugar, and applesauce and mix well with a hand mixer or food processor. Add the flour and Grape-Nuts and mix. Blend in the date mixture.

3. Pour into the prepared loaf pan. Bake for 1 hour 10 minutes.

Makes 12 servings

One serving contains: 227 calories, .3g of fat

Blueberry-Bran Bread

Deep, dark, and heavy, this highly nutritious loaf fits in well at breakfast. It is best served warm from the oven, topped with Honey Butter Spread (page 162) or light cream cheese.

1 cup boiling water	2 teaspoons vanilla extract
1 1/2 teaspoons baking soda	2 cups flour
1/3 cup chopped dates	1 teaspoon salt
4 egg whites	1 cup All-Bran
1 cup sugar	1/2 cup frozen blueberries (not thawed)
1/3 cup plus 2 tablespoons unsweetened applesauce	

1. Preheat the oven to 325°F. Coat a 9 × 5-inch loaf pan with nonstick spray and set aside.

2. In a medium bowl mix together the boiling water, baking soda, and dates and set aside to cool.

3. In a large bowl beat together the egg whites and sugar. Add the applesauce and vanilla extract and blend until smooth. Stir in the flour, salt, and All-Bran.

4. Pour half the batter into the prepared pan. Place half the blueberries evenly over the top of the batter. Pour the rest of the batter into the pan over the blueberries. Spread the remaining blueberries evenly over the top.

5. Bake for 55 to 65 minutes or until a toothpick inserted into the center comes out clean. Cool for 5 minutes and remove from the pan.

Makes 12 servings

One serving contains: 181 calories, .5g of fat

Golden Poke 'n' Pour Gingerbread

This deep mahogany bread assaults the senses with a wealth of spices. Delicately sweetened with honey, it is moist and not overly rich. Holes are poked in the batter with a fork so that the glaze can seep into the bread.

2 1/4 cups flour

1 teaspoon baking soda

1 teaspoon baking powder

1/2 teaspoon salt

1 tablespoon ground ginger

1/2 teaspoon cinnamon

1/2 cup Smart Beat margarine

1/2 cup dark brown sugar, packed

1/2 cup light brown sugar, packed

4 egg whites

1/3 cup light sour cream

2/3 cup buttermilk

Glaze:

3/4 cup sugar

2 tablespoons Smart Beat margarine, melted

1/3 cup evaporated skim milk

1 teaspoon vanilla extract

1. Preheat the oven to 350°F. Coat a 9-inch square baking pan with nonstick spray and set aside.

2. Combine the flour, baking soda, baking powder, salt, ginger, and cinnamon and set aside.

3. In a large bowl cream the margarine and brown sugars about 3 minutes or until smooth. Add the egg whites and mix well. Beat in the sour cream and buttermilk. Blend in dry ingredients until smooth.

4. Pour the batter into the prepared pan and bake for 35 to 40 minutes or until a toothpick inserted into the bread comes out clean. Cool.

5. Using a fork, poke all around the top of the bread about 25 times.

6. To make glaze: In a small bowl combine the margarine, evaporated skim milk, sugar, and vanilla extract and mix until smooth. Pour the glaze over the top of the bread.

Makes 16 servings

One serving contains: 185 calories, 2.1g of fat

Pumpkin Bread

This sweet, spicy, and rich golden harvest bread is great for the holidays, besides being extra nutritious. Pumpkin is loaded with vitamin A.

7 egg whites

2 cups sugar

3/4 cup unsweetened applesauce

2 cups canned pumpkin

2 cups flour

2 teaspoons baking powder

1 teaspoon baking soda

3/4 teaspoon salt

2 teaspoons cinnamon

1 teaspoon pumpkin pie spice

1. Preheat the oven to 350°F. Coat an 8½ × 4½-inch loaf pan with nonstick spray and set aside.

2. In a large bowl beat the egg whites until foamy. Add the sugar, applesauce, and pumpkin and beat at medium speed. Add the flour, baking powder, baking soda, salt, cinnamon, and pumpkin pie spice and mix at low speed for 3 to 4 minutes.

3. Fill the prepared loaf pan with the batter. Bake for 1 hour or until a toothpick inserted into the center comes out clean.

Makes 12 servings

One serving contains: 246 calories, .4g of fat

Cookies

I love sweets of all kinds, but if I were allowed to choose only one and eat it for all eternity I would pick cookies. It sounds a little corny, but my first experience in the kitchen was baking a batch of homemade chocolate chip cookies with my grandmother. (That is probably how everyone else started baking too.) They were full of real butter and loaded with chocolate chips, and we ate them hot out of the oven. I was hooked.

What is it that I love about cookies? Their density, their richness, their individual size, and especially their versatility. You can make cookies hard or soft, or light as air as with meringues, or decadently rich as with my double chocolate-chip fudge. Most recipes are inherently simple—just mix, drop on the pan, and bake. The one important trick to baking good cookies is to be accurate in your measurement of the ingredients. If the recipe calls for a cup, make sure it is a level cup. When using brown sugar, always pack the cup before leveling it. The same goes for tablespoons and other measures; always carefully level them.

How can my cookies be lower in fat yet taste so good? First, I cut the fat down to the absolute minimum that will allow them to retain superior taste. With a few types of cookies, the fat can be eliminated entirely. But in most cases some fat is still required to carry the taste and texture. On the other hand, this is not nearly as much as is customarily loaded into a normal cookie. I use only egg whites because the yolks are laden with cholesterol and do not generally add enough to the taste to justify their health penalty.

The great majority of the ingredients in my cookies are the same as in normal cookies: white flour, white sugar, brown sugar, and so on. These allow me to retain the familiar cookie flavors of which most of us are so fond. I try to augment the taste by adding extra amounts of flavor-rich ingredients like Dutch cocoa, vanilla, cinnamon, ground graham crackers, and ground vanilla wafers. In lieu of nuts I use Grape-Nuts, Rice Krispies, or rolled oats. If I cannot eliminate the nuts entirely, I use greatly reduced quantities since a little can go a long way toward adding flavor. I have found that when I start using "health food" ingredients such as whole wheat flour, sugar substitutes, and reduced-sodium products, the taste of the cookies is so drastically altered that they are hardly worth eating.

Here are some tips that will be helpful when you make cookies:

BAKING

- Make the cookies as similar as possible in size and thickness. This will allow them to bake uniformly.

- Use a cool cookie sheet. A hot one will soften the dough, make it spread, and change its baking characteristics.

- Bake one sheet of cookies at a time, placing it in the center of the rack. Multiple sheets placed in different positions on the rack will bake unevenly.

- Monitor the cookies starting at the minimum baking time. It does not take more than a minute or two of extra baking to make a big difference in your cookies.

- Unless the recipe states differently, remove your cookies from the hot cookie sheet with a spatula as soon as possible after baking and cool them on a wire rack. Otherwise they continue to cook. Always cool them completely before storage.

STORING

- To store soft cookies, place them in an airtight container. This will keep them moist. Placing a piece of bread or apple in the container will also help them stay moist. Just check the bread or apple periodically and, if it gets old, replace it.

Double Chocolate-Chip Fudge Cookies

Usually this recipe is loaded with butter and whole eggs. I still use unsweetened chocolate to give it a melt-in-your-mouth taste, but have greatly cut the fat with reduced-fat margarine and corn syrup. These cookies are so rich they taste more like a piece of fudge than a cookie.

4 ounces unsweetened chocolate	5 egg whites
1/4 cup Smart Beat margarine	2 cups flour
1/4 cup corn syrup	2 teaspoons baking powder
2 cups sugar	1/2 teaspoon salt
2 teaspoons vanilla extract	1/3 cup powdered sugar for coating

1. Preheat the oven to 350°F. Line a cookie sheet with parchment paper or coat with nonstick spray and set aside.

2. Put the chocolate and margarine into a large bowl and melt them in a microwave oven. Blend in the corn syrup and sugar with a hand mixer and let the mixture cool slightly. Add the vanilla extract and egg whites and mix well. Add the flour, baking powder, and salt and mix well. Chill the dough for at least 30 minutes.

3. Shape the dough into 1-inch balls. To coat the cookies, place the powdered sugar in a small bowl and roll the cookies, coating heavily.

4. Place the balls 2 inches apart on the prepared cookie sheet. Bake for about 15 minutes. The outside should just be starting to harden and crack. The inside should still be somewhat raw. (As with the Superfudgy Brownie on page 94, underbaking is the key to the fudgy taste and consistency of this cookie. Overbake these cookies and they will become dry and lose their fudgy taste. They need to be slightly raw in the middle.) Allow cookies to cool and remove them from the cookie sheet.

Makes 48 cookies

One cookie contains: 72 calories, 1.5g of fat

Chocolate Chip Cookies

A plate of fresh-baked chocolate chip cookies hot from the oven is a comforting way to welcome your children home after a day at school. Most chocolate chip cookies rely on the chocolate chips to give the cookie its characteristic flavor. Here, the batter itself is so good that you can use only ⅓ cup of chocolate chips for the entire recipe. Keep lots of milk close at hand—nonfat, of course.

7 tablespoons corn oil margarine, softened

2 tablespoons water

3/4 cup dark brown sugar, packed

1/4 cup sugar

2 egg whites

1 1/2 teaspoons vanilla extract

1 3/4 cups flour

1 teaspoon baking soda

1/2 teaspoon salt

1/3 cup plus 2 tablespoons minichocolate chips

1. Preheat the oven to 350°F. Line a cookie sheet with parchment paper or coat with nonstick spray and set aside.

2. In a large bowl cream together the margarine, water, brown sugar, and sugar with a hand mixer. Add the egg whites and vanilla extract and mix well. Blend in the flour, baking soda, and salt and mix well. Add the chocolate chips and blend them into the batter.

3. Scoop out the cookies in rounded ½ teaspoonfuls and place 1 inch apart on the prepared cookie sheet. Bake for 12 to 14 minutes. (They will become crispy when cooled.)

4. Remove the cookies from the oven and immediately flatten them slightly with the bottom of a glass.

Makes 125 cookies

One cookie contains: 25 calories, .8g of fat

Snickerdoodles

This cookie brings to mind the serenity of good times gone by. I recall spending pleasant afternoons looking over my grandmother's shoulder as she baked these classic cookies, and then licking the spoon. The batter tasted almost as good as the cookie. These low-fat Snickerdookles retain the old-fashioned flavor of home-made sugar cookies with a hint of cinnamon.

1 1/2 cups sifted all-purpose flour	1 tablespoon water
1 teaspoon cream of tartar	1 teaspoon vanilla extract
1/2 teaspoon baking soda	1 1/2 cups plus 3 tablespoons sugar
1/4 teaspoon salt	2 egg whites
1/2 cup (1 stick) corn oil margarine, softened	2 teaspoons ground cinnamon

1. Preheat the oven to 375°F. Line a cookie sheet with parchment paper or coat with nonstick spray and set aside.

2. In a small bowl sift together the flour, cream of tartar, baking soda, and salt and set aside. In a large bowl cream the margarine, water, vanilla extract, and 1½ cups sugar together until the mixture is light and fluffy. Beat in the egg whites. Add in the flour mixture and mix thoroughly. Refrigerate for at least 1 hour.

3. In a small bowl mix the cinnamon and 3 tablespoons of sugar. Scoop the batter into rounded ½ teaspoonfuls and roll these in the cinnamon/sugar mixture until they are well coated. Place on the prepared cookie sheet.

4. Bake the cookies for 10 to 12 minutes. Remove the cookies from the cookie sheet to cool. (They will become crispy when cooled.)

Makes 110 cookies

One cookie contains: 26 calories, .8g of fat

Chocolate Fudge Decadence

This cookie does not look nearly as rich as it is. It is dark, so no one would mistake it for vanilla, but the chocolate aftertaste is surprisingly powerful and lingers in your mouth long after the cookie is gone. The secret of this decadent, fudgy taste is rich Dutch cocoa and lots of it. Most low-fat chocolate cookie recipes simply add a few tablespoons of cocoa to the normal allotment of flour. The result is only a hint of chocolate and you leave feeling vaguely cheated. I replace almost half of the flour with cocoa. You won't feel cheated now!

High-fat versions of this recipe call for nuts. My secret in this case is Rice Krispies as a replacement. This results in an unusual cookie with an opulent, almost obscenely rich taste, but with a light and crunchy texture.

3/4 cup sifted flour

3/4 cup unsweetened Dutch cocoa

1 teaspoon baking soda

1 teaspoon ground cinnamon

1/2 cup (1 stick) corn oil margarine, softened

3 tablespoons water

3/4 cup dark brown sugar, firmly packed

3/4 cup sugar

2 egg whites

1 teaspoon vanilla extract

1 1/2 cups Rice Krispies

1. Preheat the oven to 350°F. Line a cookie sheet with parchment paper or coat with nonstick spray and set aside.

2. Sift together the flour, cocoa, baking soda, and cinnamon and set aside.

3. Cream the margarine, water, and both sugars for about 2 minutes or until smooth. Mix in the egg whites and vanilla extract. Add the dry ingredients and blend well. Stir in the Rice Krispies until well mixed. Cover and refrigerate for at least 1 hour or until firm.

4. Place rounded ½ teaspoonfuls of dough on the prepared cookie sheet, about 4 across and 6 down.

5. Bake for 14 to 16 minutes or until set. The cookies will become crispy when cooled. Repeat with the remaining dough until it is used up.

Makes 112 cookies

One cookies contains: 24 calories, .9g of fat

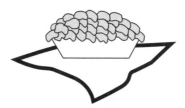

Old-World Spice Cookies

I hesitated calling this cookie a "spice" cookie. This word turns some people off. But it is nothing at all like a gingersnap, which most people envision when they hear the term spice cookie. Like a gingersnap, this cookie draws some of its sweetness from molasses, a sugar cane or sugar beet product that has not undergone the complete refining process. But unlike a gingersnap, it is rolled in sugar and baked till still moist and delicately soft. Its dusky, winter-brown color attracts the eye as its cinnamon and allspice aroma stimulates the palate. And it's a great addition to the family cookie jar because it lasts so long when kept airtight.

5 tablespoons corn oil margarine, softened

4 tablespoons Smart Beat margarine

3/4 cup sugar

1 tablespoon water

2 egg whites

1/4 cup unsulphured molasses

2 cups flour

2 teaspoons baking soda

1/2 teaspoon salt

1 tablespoon ground allspice

1 tablespoon ground cinnamon

1/3 cup sugar for coating

1. Preheat the oven to 350°F. Line a cookie sheet with parchment paper or coat with nonstick spray and set aside.

2. In a large bowl cream the margarines, sugar, and water for 2 minutes or until smooth. Beat in the egg whites. Pour in the molasses and mix well. Stir in the flour, baking soda, salt, allspice, and cinnamon and mix thoroughly. Refrigerate the batter for at least 1 hour or until it becomes firm and easy to handle.

3. Pour the sugar for coating into a small bowl. Drop the dough in rounded ½ tea-spoonfuls into the bowl of sugar and coat well. Place 2 inches apart on the prepared cookie sheet.

4. Bake for 12 to 14 minutes or until set.

Makes 96 cookies

One cookie contains: 27 calories, .7g of fat

Oat-Bran Thumbprint Cookies

Oat bran was in fashion a few years ago as a cure for everything from heart disease to bunions, and it seems to be making a comeback. Even so, working with oat bran in baked products can be difficult. It has a harsh and somewhat bitter taste when compared to a high-quality baking flour. Nonetheless, oat bran does reduce serum cholesterol and is a wonderful source of dietary fiber—if you can get it to taste good. Here I have overcome the difficulties and produced a delectable cookie that your kids can down in large quantities while you stand by feeling good about their nutrition. And since I happen to be a compulsive sweets-eater, I enjoy making a breakfast of these healthy morsels.

3/4 cup light corn syrup	1 cup flour
1/2 cup light brown sugar, packed	1 cup oat bran
1 teaspoon vanilla extract	1/2 cup quick-cooking oats
2 egg whites	1/4 teaspoon salt

Coating:

1/4 cup Grape-Nuts

3 tablespoons sugar

2 tablespoons oat bran

Filling:

1/2 cup light boysenberry, raspberry, or apricot preserves

1. Preheat the oven to 350°F. Line a cookie sheet with parchment paper or coat with nonstick spray and set aside.

2. In a large bowl combine the corn syrup, brown sugar, vanilla extract, and egg whites and mix until smooth. Add the flour, oat bran, oats, and salt, and beat until the dough is well mixed. Set aside.

3. To make coating: In a small bowl mix together the Grape-Nuts, 3 tablespoons sugar, and 2 tablespoons oat bran until well combined. Shape the prepared dough into 1-inch balls and roll in the coating mixture.

4. Place the balls 2 inches apart on the prepared cookie sheet. Press your thumb into the center of each cookie to form a well. Spoon 1 teaspoon of light preserves into each well.

5. Bake for 10 to 12 minutes or until light golden.

Makes 100 cookies

One cookie contains: 24 calories, .1g of fat

Graham Cracker Cookies

Graham crackers have that nostalgic flavor of good times gone by. Even better, they are naturally low in fat. Here I have replaced some of the flour in my standard cookie batter with ground-up graham cracker crumbs, which impart their characteristic taste to this soft, moist cookie.

5 tablespoons margarine

2 tablespoons water

1/2 cup dark brown sugar, packed

1/2 cup sugar

2 egg whites

1/2 cup plus 1 tablespoon graham cracker crumbs

2 teaspoons vanilla extract

1 1/3 cups flour

1/2 teaspoon salt

1/2 teaspoon baking powder

1/4 teaspoon baking soda

Coating:

3/4 cup graham cracker crumbs

1/2 cup sugar

1. Preheat the oven to 350°F. Line a cookie sheet with parchment paper or coat with nonstick spray and set aside.

2. Cream together the margarine, water, and sugars. Add the egg whites and mix well. Add the graham cracker crumbs and vanilla extract and mix well. Add the flour, salt, baking powder, and baking soda and combine well. Cover with plastic wrap and refrigerate for at least 1 hour for easier handling.

3. To make coating: In a medium bowl combine the graham cracker crumbs and sugar. Scoop out rounded ½-teaspoon-sized cookies from the refrigerated cookie dough and roll them in the prepared graham cracker and sugar mixture. Drop them onto the prepared cookie sheet 1 inch apart.

4. Bake for 12 to 14 minutes or until light golden.

Makes 60 cookies

One cookie contains: 46 calories, 1.2g of fat

Chocolate Graham Cracker Cookies

This cookie has that familiar and lovely flavor of graham crackers and chocolate, and they call out for a cold glass of milk. The essence of the cookie is the taste of graham crackers, while the chocolate acts as a subtle condiment.

5 tablespoons margarine

2 tablespoons water

2/3 cup dark brown sugar, packed

1/3 cup sugar

2 egg whites

1/2 cup plus 1 tablespoon chocolate graham cracker crumbs

1 teaspoon vanilla extract

1 1/3 cups flour

1 tablespoon unsweetened Dutch cocoa

1/2 teaspoon salt

1/2 teaspoon baking powder

1/4 teaspoon baking soda

Coating:

3/4 cup chocolate graham cracker crumbs, ground in a blender or food processor

1/2 cup sugar

1. Preheat the oven to 350°F. Line a cookie sheet with parchment paper or coat with nonstick spray and set aside.

2. Cream together the margarine, water, and sugars. Add the egg whites and mix well. Add the chocolate graham cracker crumbs and vanilla extract and mix well. Add the flour, cocoa, salt, baking powder, and baking soda and combine well. Cover with plastic wrap and refrigerate for at least 1 hour for easier handling.

3. To make coating: In a medium bowl combine the ground chocolate graham cracker crumbs and sugar. Scoop out rounded ½-teaspoon-sized cookies from the refrigerated cookie dough and roll them in the prepared graham cracker and sugar mixture.

4. Drop them onto the prepared cookie sheet 1 inch apart. Bake for 12 to 14 minutes or until light golden.

Makes 60 cookies

One cookie contains: 48 calories, 1.3g of fat

Butterscotch Pillows

This is a good cookie for company because it is so attractive. Rolled in powdered sugar, the cookie cracks a little as it bakes, producing a decorative "pillowy" look. It is a mixture of textures, soft inside but with the surprising crunch of Rice Krispies. Its potent butterscotch flavor comes from combining margarine with rich, dark brown sugar.

5 tablespoons margarine

2 tablespoons water

1 cup dark brown sugar, packed

2 egg whites

1 teaspoon vanilla extract

1 1/2 cups flour

1/2 teaspoon salt

1/2 teaspoon baking powder

1/4 teaspoon baking soda

1/2 cup Rice Krispies

1/2 cup plus 2 tablespoons powdered sugar for coating

1. Preheat the oven to 350°F. Line a cookie sheet with parchment paper or coat with nonstick spray and set aside.

2. Cream the margarine, water, and brown sugar until smooth. Add the egg whites and vanilla extract and mix until smooth. Add the flour, salt, baking powder, and baking soda and mix until smooth. Fold in the Rice Krispies.

3. Place the batter in the freezer for 15 to 20 minutes until firm for easier handling.

4. Place the powdered sugar in a small bowl and set aside. Form the cookies into rounded ½-teaspoon sizes and roll them in the powdered sugar to coat. Place onto cookie sheet and slightly flatten with a fork.

5. Bake for 12 minutes.

Makes 80 cookies

One cookie contains: 29 calories, .7g of fat

Brown Sugar Cookies

This is a new twist on that old favorite, sugar cookies. Traditional varieties use all white sugar; these feature brown sugar, which adds a delicate caramel flavor.

1/4 cup corn oil margarine	1 1/4 cups plus 2 tablespoons flour
1/4 cup Smart Beat margarine	1/4 teaspoon salt
1 cup light brown sugar, packed	1/4 teaspoon baking soda
2 egg whites	1/2 cup sugar for coating
1 teaspoon vanilla extract	

1. Preheat the oven to 350°F. Line a cookie sheet with parchment paper or coat with nonstick spray and set aside.

2. In a large bowl cream the margarines until smooth. Add the brown sugar and mix well. Add the egg whites and vanilla extract and mix well. Add the flour, salt, and baking soda and mix well. Refrigerate the dough for at least 1 hour until it is firm and easy to handle.

3. Place the sugar in a small bowl. Drop the dough by rounded ½ teaspoonfuls into the bowl of sugar and roll to coat. Place the dough on the prepared cookie sheet about 2 inches apart.

4. Bake for 12 to 15 minutes or until golden brown. (They will become crispy when cooled.)

Makes 80 cookies

One cookie contains: 29 calories, .7g of fat

Chocolate Sugar Cookies

Classic sugar cookies, which are normally vanilla based, have long been a family favorite. Since my family loves chocolate, I developed this chocolate adaptation, which features a healthy dose of unsweetened cocoa and is even better. Unlike some of the other chocolate cookies in this chapter that are fudgy and dense, these are light and crunchy. This may be unfortunate because you will be tempted to eat a lot of them!

7 tablespoons corn oil margarine, softened

2 tablespoons water

1 1/2 cups sugar

2 egg whites

1 teaspoon vanilla extract

1 cup flour

1/2 cup unsweetened Dutch cocoa

1/4 teaspoon salt

1/2 teaspoon baking soda

1/3 cup sugar for coating

1. Preheat the oven to 350°F. Line a cookie sheet with parchment paper or coat with nonstick spray and set aside.

2. In a large bowl cream the margarine and water until smooth. Add the sugar and mix for about 2 minutes. Stir in the egg whites and vanilla extract. Mix in the flour, cocoa, salt, and baking soda and beat until smooth. Refrigerate the dough for at least 1 hour until it is firm and easy to handle.

3. Place the sugar in a small bowl. Drop the dough by rounded ½ teaspoonfuls into the bowl of sugar and roll to coat.

4. Place on the prepared cookie sheet about 2 inches apart. Bake for 12 to 15 minutes or until golden. (They will become crispy when cooled.)

Makes 100 cookies

One cookie contains: 27 calories, .9g of fat

Oatmeal Lace Cookies

This golden brown lace cookie is an oatmeal lover's delight. I have replaced all the flour with oatmeal and all the sugar with dark brown sugar. What results is a light, brittle, and highly textured cookie that tastes incredibly rich. The potent mixture of vanilla, oatmeal, and dark brown sugar creates a delicate flavor with a strong hint of caramel. And they make a great accompaniment for your favorite low-fat yogurt or ice cream.

2 cups rolled oats

1 cup dark brown sugar, firmly packed

1 teaspoon baking powder

1/2 teaspoon cinnamon

4 tablespoons corn oil margarine, melted

3 tablespoons Smart Beat margarine, melted

2 egg whites

1. Preheat the oven to 350°F. Line a cookie sheet with parchment paper or coat with nonstick spray and set aside.

2. In a medium bowl mix together the oats, brown sugar, baking powder, and cinnamon. Add the margarines and mix well. Add the egg whites and mix well.

3. Drop the batter by rounded ½ teaspoonfuls onto the prepared baking sheet. Bake for 8 to 10 minutes or until golden brown.

Makes 100 cookies

One cookie contains: 19 calories, .6g of fat

Meringues: The Guilt-Free Cookies

For anyone who is concerned with fat intake, meringue is a wondrous find. Most people have had plenty of experience with meringues over the years, but few people realize that meringues are one of those incredibly rare items that are naturally low in fat and actually taste good! You don't have to alter the recipes for meringues to make them low-fat and delicious. They are and always have been virtually fat-free.

On top of it they are a little like cotton candy, in that they are larger and more satisfying than you would expect from the actual weight and amount of their ingredients. Meringues are light, fluffy, and, like cotton candy, melt in your mouth. They are crunchy on the outside yet bursting with flavor. You can eat twenty of them, enough to fill a huge plate to overflowing, and still take in no fat and only 150 calories. You can experience the rare pleasure of seeming to pig out, while actually eating moderately. It's almost too good to be true.

I have worked with two basic recipes, vanilla and chocolate, and have developed a number of delectable variations. But no matter what the flavor, all meringues have a foundation of egg whites and sugar. They are beaten until fluffy to trap air in the mixture and then baked into a hard, porous structure, somewhat resembling honeycomb. I bake them on low heat for about 40 minutes and then leave them in the warm oven overnight. This removes all the moisture and yields a uniform cookie that is firm throughout. Other baking methods may produce brittle meringues in which the crust flakes off and they fall apart.

But in any case, I like to make them small and bite-sized. This allows you to pop the entire cookie into your mouth at once. Otherwise it has the tendency to shatter into millions of little pieces and become troublesome. You will find yourself scraping the tiny remnants into little piles and then trying to figure out how to get them into your mouth rather than down the front of your shirt.

Vanilla Meringue Cookies

These clean-tasting, snowy little nuggets can be consumed virtually without end. With a glass of milk or a cup of coffee they leave you feeling satisfied after a meal, but not stuffed. And the flawless vanilla flavor lingers long after the last morsel is gone.

3 egg whites	**1/2 teaspoon cream of tartar**
1/8 teaspoon salt	**3/4 cup sugar**

1. Preheat the oven to 250°F. Line a cookie sheet with parchment paper or coat with nonstick spray and set aside.

2. In a medium bowl beat the egg whites until foamy. Add the salt and cream of tartar and beat until stiff peaks form. It should look like marshmallow cream. Add the sugar 1 tablespoon at a time and beat until glossy and smooth.

3. Drop the batter onto the prepared cookie sheet by teaspoonfuls. They can be placed close together but not touching because they don't spread.

4. Bake for 40 minutes. Turn off the oven and do not open the oven door. Allow to cool in the closed oven for 3 hours or, for best results, overnight.

Makes 95 cookies

One cookie contains: 7 calories, 0g of fat

Chocolate Meringues

These chocolatey little goblets are very hard to stop eating once you start. The addition of ground-up chocolate chips to the batter enriches the flavor and gives you something to look forward to as you chew them, a little like the chocolate chips do in a chocolate chip cookie.

3 egg whites

1/8 teaspoon salt

1/2 teaspoon cream of tartar

3/4 cup sugar

3 tablespoons unsweetened Dutch cocoa

2 tablespoons ground minichocolate chips (can grind in blender)

1. Preheat the oven to 250°F. Line a cookie sheet with parchment paper or coat with nonstick spray and set aside.

2. In a large bowl beat the egg whites until foamy. Add the salt and cream of tartar. Continue beating until stiff peaks form. It should look like marshmallow cream. Add the sugar 1 tablespoon at a time and beat until glossy and smooth. On a low speed mix in the cocoa 1 tablespoon at a time. Mix in the ground chocolate chips.

3. Drop the batter by teaspoonfuls onto the prepared cookie sheet. The cookies do not rise or spread much, so they can be placed close together but not touching.

4. Bake for 40 minutes. Do not open the oven. Instead, turn it off and allow the cookies to cool in the closed oven for at least 3 hours or, for best results, overnight. Store in an airtight container.

Makes 95 cookies

One cookie contains: 9 calories, .1g of fat

Lemon Meringue Cookies

These light cookies, exuding the citrusy aroma of fresh lemon and slightly tangy to the palate, are so good that my husband and I ate an entire tray of them during our taste-testing session. We simply couldn't stop. These are surefire winners!

3 egg whites

1/8 teaspoon salt

1/2 teaspoon cream of tartar

1/2 cup plus 3 tablespoons sugar

2 tablespoons instant lemon pudding mix

1. Preheat the oven to 250°F. Line a cookie sheet with parchment paper or coat with nonstick spray and set aside.

2. Beat the egg whites until foamy. Add the salt and cream of tartar and continue beating until stiff peaks form. Stir in the sugar, 1 tablespoon at a time, and mix on low speed until smooth. Fold in the lemon pudding mix on slow speed.

3. Drop the batter onto the prepared cookie sheet by teaspoonfuls. They can be placed close together but not touching because they do not spread.

4. Bake for 40 minutes. Do not open the oven door. Turn off the oven and allow the cookies to cool in the closed oven for at least 3 hours or, for best results, overnight.

Makes 80 cookies

One cookie contains: 8 calories, 0g of fat

English Toffee Meringues

This is a very rich meringue. Although it has a little more fat than most meringues because of the English toffee bits, it is also chewy, particularly substantial in texture, and satisfying. It is not at all your typical meringue.

3 egg whites

1/8 teaspoon salt

1/2 teaspoon cream of tartar

3/4 cup sugar

2 1/2 tablespoons ground vanilla wafer crumbs

2 tablespoons English toffee bits (found in the baking section of the market)

1. Preheat the oven to 250°F. Line a cookie sheet with parchment paper or coat with nonstick spray and set aside.

2. In a large bowl beat the egg whites until foamy. Add the salt and cream of tartar and continue to beat until stiff peaks form. Gradually stir in the sugar. Gently fold in the vanilla wafer crumbs and toffee bits.

3. Drop the batter onto the prepared cookie sheet by teaspoonfuls. Since these cookies do not rise or spread, they can be dropped close together but not touching.

4. Bake for 40 minutes. Do not open the oven door. Turn off the oven and leave the cookies in the closed oven to cool for at least 3 hours or, for best results, overnight.

Makes 100 cookies

One cookie contains: 8 calories, .8g of fat

Coconut-Graham Meringues

Because of the added graham cracker crumbs and shredded coconut these meringues are more substantial than most, like the English Toffee Meringues (page 68). And it takes surprisingly small amounts of coconut and graham crackers to profoundly dominate the flavor of the cookie.

3 egg whites	3/4 cup sugar
1/8 teaspoon salt	2 tablespoons graham cracker crumbs
1/2 teaspoon cream of tartar	2 tablespoons shredded coconut

1. Preheat the oven to 250°F. Line a cookie sheet with parchment paper or coat with nonstick spray and set aside.

2. In a large bowl beat the egg whites until foamy. Add the salt and cream of tartar and continue to beat until stiff peaks form. Gradually stir in the sugar. Fold in the graham cracker crumbs and coconut.

3. Drop the batter onto the prepared cookie sheet by rounded ½ teaspoonfuls. They can be dropped close together but not touching because they do not spread or rise.

4. Bake for 40 minutes. Do not open the oven door. Turn off the oven and allow the cookies to cool in the closed oven for at least 3 hours or, for best results, overnight.

Makes 100 cookies

One cookie contains: 7 calories, .1g of fat

Chocolate Meringue Nests

These light cocoa cookies are formed into large, sturdy, hollowed-out nests to create an elegant serving dish for ice cream or yogurt. When filled with your favorite frozen dessert (I usually opt for nonfat vanilla or chocolate yogurt) and topped with fresh berries, they are simple and elegant.

1/4 cup powdered sugar

1/4 cup unsweetened Dutch cocoa

3 egg whites

1/8 teaspoon cream of tartar

3/4 cup sugar

1. Preheat the oven to 250°F. Line a cookie sheet with parchment paper or coat with nonstick spray.

2. In a small bowl sift the powdered sugar and cocoa together and set the mixture aside. In a large bowl beat the egg whites with an electric mixer until frothy. Add the cream of tartar and beat on high speed until soft peaks form. Add the granulated sugar 1 tablespoon at a time, continuously beating until the meringue forms stiff peaks and is glossy with the consistency of marshmallow cream. On low speed, slowly beat in the cocoa mixture, mixing until well blended.

3. Drop the meringue batter by large spoonfuls into six 3-inch-wide mounds onto the prepared cookie sheet. Make a well in each mound with the back of a spoon and push up the sides to form a nest.

4. Bake for 1 hour. Do not open the oven. Turn off the oven and let the meringues cool in the closed oven for at least 3 hours or, for best results, overnight.

5. To serve, fill with ice cream or yogurt and top with a few spoonfuls of your favorite fresh berries.

Makes 6 cookies

One cookie contains: 133 calories, .5g of fat

Biscotti

Biscotti is the Italian name for "twice-baked" cookies. They are baked the first time as a log, then sliced and baked again. Although they have been around for generations, biscotti, also known as "mandelbrot," became a hot item in the '90s with the growth in popularity of coffee houses. More recently the cookies have lost a little panache because they are usually loaded with fat, baked hard enough to put one's molars at risk, and are often somewhat tasteless. Regular biscotti are simply not good enough to warrant the heavy fat and calorie intake.

But these low-fat versions are different. They are still perfect dipping cookies with your favorite cup of coffee or tea, but they are light, sweeter than normal, and loaded with subtle flavors. And they contain substantially less than half of the normal biscotti fat content, as well as having no cholesterol, egg yolks, or butter.   .

I have included a wide variety of biscotti recipes. Although my family and friends all have their favorites, my own favorites are the poppy seed and the cinnamon chocolate chip varieties. Keep them in an airtight container and they will remain fresh for several months. I state this with some confidence because they will all be eaten before you get a chance to test this theory.

Poppy Seed Biscotti

Deeply textured and covered with fluffy white powdered sugar, these festive and beautiful cookies bring to mind holiday seasons, snowy afternoons, crackling fires, and steaming cups of rich coffee. (Confession: Having been born and raised in Southern California, I have, unfortunately, no personal experience with such scenes. I am, however, not without some authority because I have seen Bing Crosby in White Christmas *and* Holiday Inn *more times than I care to count.)*

I have found that most people who claim that they don't like poppy seeds still love this cookie. Poppy seeds can be slightly harsh in taste, almost bitter, if you use too many of them. But in proper quantity and combined with the sweetness of powdered sugar they impart a distinctive nutty flavor and home-baked taste.

6 egg whites	2 teaspoons baking powder
1/2 cup canola oil	1/4 teaspoon salt
2 teaspoons vanilla extract	2 tablespoons poppy seeds
1 cup sugar	1/2 cup powdered sugar for topping
3 cups flour	

1. Preheat the oven to 350°F. Line a baking sheet with parchment paper or coat with nonstick spray and set aside.

2. In a large bowl blend together the egg whites and oil. Add the vanilla extract and sugar and mix well. Add the flour, baking powder, and salt and mix until well combined. Add the poppy seeds and mix until the dough is combined. (Do not overmix.)

3. Divide the dough into 4 portions. Shape each portion into a loaf 2 inches wide and 1 inch high. Place the loaves 2 inches apart on the prepared baking sheet. Bake for 20 to 25 minutes or until golden brown.

4. Remove the pan from the oven and transfer the loaves to a cutting board using a spatula. Cut the loaves crosswise into ¼-inch slices. Place the slices on the baking sheet.

5. Return the sliced loaves to the oven and bake for 10 minutes. Turn the biscotti over and bake another 10 minutes.

6. While still slightly warm, dust both sides of each biscotto with powdered sugar.

Makes 120 biscotti

One biscotto contains: 28 calories, 1.0g of fat

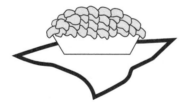

Chocolate Biscotti

For chocolate lovers who need to dip their cookies, these dark biscotti, covered with glittering crystals of granulated sugar, will work admirably. The chocolate flavor is more subtle than that of most heavy-duty chocolate cookies, so it will not overpower the aroma of your favorite hot beverage. And like all the biscotti in this book, the light flavor leaves a fresh, pleasant taste in your mouth.

6 egg whites	3 cups flour
1/2 cup canola oil	2 teaspoons baking powder
1 teaspoon vanilla extract	1/4 teaspoon salt
1 cup sugar	1/4 cup minichocolate chips
1/2 cup unsweetened Dutch cocoa	1/2 cup sugar for topping

1. Preheat the oven to 350°F. Line a baking sheet with parchment paper or coat with nonstick spray and set aside.

2. In a large bowl blend together the egg whites and oil. Add the vanilla extract and sugar and mix well. Add the cocoa, flour, baking powder, and salt and mix until combined. Add the minichocolate chips and mix until blended. (Do not overmix.)

3. Divide the dough into 4 portions. Shape each portion into a loaf 2 inches wide and 1 inch high. Place the loaves 2 inches apart on the prepared baking sheet. Bake for 20 to 25 minutes or until golden brown.

4. Remove the pan from the oven and transfer the loaves to a cutting board using a spatula. Cut the loaves crosswise into ¼-inch slices. Place the slices on the baking sheet. Sprinkle a light sugar topping over each slice.

5. Return the sliced loaves to the oven and bake for 10 minutes or until lightly browned. Remove from the oven, turn the slices over, and sprinkle the remaining sugar over each slice. Bake for an additional 10 minutes.

Makes 125 biscotti

One biscotto contains: 30 calories, 1.1g of fat

Peanut Butter Biscotti

This has the most powerful and distinctive taste of all my biscotti recipes. The flavor of peanut butter dominates the other ingredients, as it tends to do in cookies. Because peanut butter has a high intrinsic oil content, I have been able to reduce the amount of canola oil added so the total fat remains relatively low.

6 egg whites

1/2 cup canola oil

1 teaspoon vanilla extract

1 cup sugar

3 cups flour

2 teaspoons baking powder

1/4 teaspoon salt

1/4 cup peanut butter chips, chopped

1/2 cup sugar for topping

1. Preheat the oven to 350°F. Line a baking sheet with parchment paper or coat with nonstick spray and set aside.

2. In a large bowl blend together the egg whites and oil. Add the vanilla extract and sugar and mix well. Add the flour, baking powder, and salt and mix until combined. Add the peanut butter chips and mix until blended.

3. Divide the dough into 4 portions. With floured hands, shape each portion into a loaf 2 inches wide and 1 inch high. Place the loaves 2 inches apart on the prepared baking sheet. Bake for 20 to 25 minutes or until golden brown.

4. Remove the pan from the oven and transfer the loaves to a cutting board using a spatula. Cut the loaves crosswise into ¼-inch slices. Place the slices on the baking sheet, cut side down. Sprinkle a light sugar topping over each slice.

5. Return the sliced loaves to the oven and bake for 10 minutes or until lightly browned. Remove from the oven, turn the slices over, and sprinkle the remaining sugar over the slices. Bake for an additional 10 minutes.

Makes 120 biscotti

One biscotto contains: 28 calories, 1.0g of fat

Almond Biscotti

This is my husband's favorite because he loves the flavor of almonds. To him, almonds in every form are wonderful. He eats Jordan almonds at the movies, buys almond M&M's instead of regular or peanut, and, despite knowing it's not socially acceptable, surreptitiously digs through bowls of mixed nuts to pick out the almonds.

6 egg whites

1/2 cup canola oil

1 teaspoon almond extract

1/2 teaspoon vanilla extract

1 cup sugar

3 cups flour

2 teaspoons baking powder

1/4 teaspoon salt

1/4 cup chopped almonds

1/2 cup sugar for topping

1. Preheat the oven to 350°F. Line a baking sheet with parchment paper or coat with nonstick spray and set aside.

2. In a large bowl blend together the egg whites and oil. Add the almond extract, vanilla extract, and sugar and mix well. Add the flour, baking powder, and salt and mix until well combined. Add the almonds and mix until the dough is blended. (Do not overmix.)

3. Divide the dough into 4 portions. With floured hands, shape each portion into a loaf 2 inches wide and 1 inch high. Place the loaves 2 inches apart on the prepared baking sheet. Bake for 20 to 25 minutes or until golden brown.

4. Remove the pan from the oven and transfer the loaves to a cutting board using a spatula. Cut the loaves crosswise into ¼-inch slices. Place the slices on the baking sheet. Sprinkle a light sugar topping over each slice.

5. Return the sliced loaves to the oven and bake for 10 minutes or until lightly browned. Turn the slices over and sprinkle the remaining sugar over the top of each slice. Return to the oven and bake for an additional 10 minutes.

Makes 120 biscotti

One biscotto contains: 27 calories, 1.0g of fat

Cinnamon Chocolate Chip Biscotti

The delightful mixture of cinnamon and chocolate chips is one of my favorite flavors, bringing to mind childhood memories of coffee cake and the family breakfast table. And when I dip it in a hot cup of coffee, some of the cinnamon dissolves, and I get a hint of cinnamon in my coffee.

6 egg whites

1/2 cup canola oil

1 teaspoon vanilla extract

1 cup sugar

3 cups flour

2 teaspoons baking powder

1/2 teaspoon cinnamon

1/4 teaspoon salt

1/4 cup minichocolate chips

Topping:

1/2 cup sugar

1 tablespoon cinnamon

1. Preheat the oven to 350°F. Line a baking sheet with parchment paper or coat with nonstick spray and set aside.

2. In a large bowl blend together the egg whites and oil. Add the vanilla extract and sugar and mix well. Add the flour, baking powder, cinnamon, and salt and mix until well combined. Add the minichocolate chips and mix until the dough is blended. (Do not overmix.)

3. Divide the dough into 4 portions. With floured hands, shape each portion into a loaf 2 inches wide and 1 inch high. Place the loaves 2 inches apart on the prepared baking sheet. Bake for 20 to 25 minutes or until golden brown.

4. Remove the pan from the oven and transfer the loaves to a cutting board using a spatula. Cut the loaves crosswise into ¼-inch slices. Place the slices on the baking sheet.

5. To make topping: In a small bowl mix the sugar and cinnamon. Sprinkle the sugar and cinnamon topping over each slice.

6. Return the sliced loaves to the oven and bake for 10 minutes or until lightly browned. Remove from the oven, turn the slices over, and sprinkle sugar and cinnamon topping over each slice. Bake for an additional 10 minutes.

Makes 120 biscotti

One biscotto contains: 27 calories, 1.0g of fat

Oatmeal-Almond Crisps

This is another cookie that uses oats rather than flour. Oats are, of course, different from flour in many ways, but two of these differences make oatmeal cookies exceptional. The first is that oats have a slightly higher fat content than flour, making cookies based on oats naturally richer. The second is the more substantial and, if baked sufficiently long, crunchy texture of oats.

These earthy, heavy cookies display both oat characteristics in abundance. They are great for breakfast or for a healthy snack between meals and would make a delicious replacement for a commercial granola bar.

The almond aroma comes from almond extract, which, compared to vanilla extract, is very powerful. I have been careful not to use too much of it because even a slight excess will overpower all the other wonderful flavors in the cookie. And if you are concerned that almonds, like all nuts, contain oil, you will be happy to note that I have used only one tablespoon of ground almonds in the recipe.

3 egg whites	**1 tablespoon finely chopped almonds**
1 cup light brown sugar, packed	**3/4 teaspoon almond extract**
2 cups rolled oats	

1. Preheat the oven to 275°F. Line a cookie sheet with parchment paper or coat with nonstick spray and set aside.

2. In a large bowl beat the egg whites until stiff. Sift in the brown sugar and mix well. Stir in the oats, almonds, and almond extract.

3. Drop the batter by rounded ½ teaspoonfuls onto the prepared cookie sheet. Bake for 30 minutes or until golden brown.

4. Carefully remove the cookies from the pan while hot, and cool on a rack. If you let them cool on the cookie sheet they will break as you try to remove them.

Makes 80 cookies

One cookie contains: 19 calories, .2g of fat

M&M Crunch Cookies

At Mrs. Beasley's, the decadent bake shop that I used to own, M&M cookies were always a great hit with kids and grown-ups alike. It wasn't so much the chocolate taste of the M&M's that attracted fans, but rather the look of them sprinkled across the top and the incredible aroma of the batter. For years I have mourned the inability to eat these cookies as a part of my healthy diet, but no more. With the advent of mini-M&M's and the use of my low-fat baking techniques, I have been able to resurrect these gems in a healthier form while retaining the look and the lavish taste of the old version.

7 tablespoons corn oil margarine

2 tablespoons water

3/4 cup dark brown sugar, packed

3/4 cup sugar

2 egg whites

2 1/2 teaspoons vanilla extract

1 3/4 cups flour

1 teaspoon baking soda

1/2 teaspoon salt

1 1/4 cups Rice Krispies

1 bag semisweet mini-M&M baking bits

1. Preheat the oven to 350°F. Line a cookie sheet with parchment paper or coat with nonstick spray and set aside.

2. In a large bowl cream the margarine, water, and both sugars for about 2 minutes or until smooth. Add the egg whites and mix well. Stir in the vanilla extract. Add the flour, baking soda, and salt and beat thoroughly. Fold in the Rice Krispies.

3. Drop the dough by rounded ½ teaspoonfuls onto the prepared cookie sheet. Place about 4 cookies across and 6 down. Press 4 mini-M&Ms into the top of each cookie. Bake for 12 to 13 minutes or until golden brown. (They will become crispy when cooled.)

Makes 115 cookies

One cookie contains: 28 calories, .9g of fat

Ranger Cookies

When I was a kid I looked forward to Friday lunch in the school cafeteria because they served one of my favorite cookies, Rangers. As a chocoholic, it was unusual for me to be particularly fond of a vanilla-based cookie, but these were loaded with flavor, stemming from the combination of oats, Rice Krispies, and coconut in a lush, buttery vanilla foundation. I have captured the essence of this delightful cookie. It is light golden in color with dimples on top and has a nutty taste from the coconut and Rice Krispies.

1 1/4 cups flour

1 teaspoon baking soda

1 1/4 teaspoons ground cinnamon

1/4 teaspoon salt

7 tablespoons corn oil margarine, softened

3 tablespoons water

3/4 cup dark brown sugar, firmly packed

3/4 cup sugar

2 egg whites

1 1/2 teaspoons vanilla extract

1 cup old-fashioned rolled oats

1 1/4 cups Rice Krispies

1/2 cup shredded coconut

1. Preheat the oven to 350°F. Line 2 cookie sheets with parchment paper or coat with nonstick spray and set aside.

2. In a medium bowl mix together the flour, baking soda, cinnamon, and salt and set aside.

3. In a large bowl cream the margarine, water, and both sugars for about 2 minutes or until smooth. Stir in the egg whites. Mix in the vanilla extract. Add the dry ingredients and mix thoroughly. Mix in the oats, Rice Krispies, and coconut and blend until smooth.

4. Place rounded ½ teaspoonfuls of dough on the prepared cookie sheets, 4 down and 6 across. Bake for 10 to 12 minutes or until slightly browned. (They will become crispy when cooled.)

Makes 120 cookies

One cookie contains: 26 calories, .8g of fat

Crispy Cornflake Cookies

These look like normal cookies, are sweet and crunchy like normal cookies, but the flavor is simultaneously mysterious and familiar. Most people will unsuccessfully struggle to identify it. The secret ingredient? Cornflakes. With the high content of oatmeal and cornflakes, these cookies are a nutritious addition to a glass of milk or cup of coffee at the breakfast table.

1/2 cup (1 stick) reduced-fat margarine (50% less fat)

1 cup sugar

2 egg whites

2 teaspoons vanilla extract

1 1/2 cups flour

1 teaspoon baking powder

1 teaspoon baking soda

1/4 teaspoon salt

1 1/4 cups oatmeal

2 cups cornflakes, crushed

1. Preheat the oven to 375°F. Line a cookie sheet with parchment paper or spray it with a nonstick spray.

2. In a large bowl cream together the margarine and sugar. Add the egg whites and vanilla extract and beat well. Add the flour, baking powder, baking soda, and salt and beat well. Stir in the oatmeal and cornflakes and mix with a spoon.

3. Drop the batter by rounded ½ teaspoonfuls onto the cookie sheet. Bake for 10 to 12 minutes or until lightly browned.

Makes 120 cookies

One cookie contains: 24 calories, .9g of fat

Coconut Macaroon Clouds

Most macaroons are heavy, rich, and very sweet. These are unusual because they are light and fluffy, like a cross between a macaroon and a meringue. They exude that well-known coconut macaroon aroma but they melt in your mouth.

2 egg whites	2/3 cup sugar
1/2 teaspoon vanilla extract	1/3 cup flaked coconut

1. Preheat the oven to 325°F. Line a cookie sheet with parchment paper or coat with nonstick spray and set aside.

2. In a medium bowl beat the egg whites and vanilla extract on high speed until soft peaks form. Gradually add the sugar, beating until stiff peaks form. Fold in the coconut.

3. Drop the mixture onto the prepared cookie sheet in rounded ½ teaspoonfuls. Bake for 15 minutes or until the edges are lightly browned. Let cookies cool.

Makes 60 cookies

One cookie contains: 16 calories, .5g of fat

Variation:

Chocolate Chip Coconut Macaroons

Sprinkle 4 semisweet minichocolate chips on top of each cookie after it has been dropped on the cookie sheet. This adds .1g of fat and 1.5 calories to each cookie. It also completely changes the taste. The combination of chocolate and coconut make this cookie taste like a lighter-than-air Mounds bar.

Chocolate Chip Macaroons

3 egg whites

1/4 teaspoon cream of tartar

1/8 teaspoon salt

3/4 cup sugar

1 teaspoon vanilla extract

1 1/2 cups flaked coconut

3 tablespoons semisweet minichocolate chips

1. Preheat the oven to 300°F. Line a cookie sheet with parchment paper or coat with nonstick spray and set aside.

2. In a medium bowl beat the egg whites, cream of tartar, and salt until foamy. Beat in the sugar 1 tablespoon at a time, and continue beating until stiff and glossy. Fold in the vanilla extract and coconut.

3. Drop the mixture onto the prepared cookie sheet by rounded ½ teaspoonfuls about 1 inch apart. Sprinkle 3 minichocolate chips on top of each cookie.

4. Bake 20 to 25 minutes or until the edges are just light brown. Cool for 15 minutes and remove from the cookie sheet.

Makes 85 cookies

One cookie contains: 17 calories, .7g of fat

Peanut Butter Chocolate Chip Cookies

Your kids will love these because the peanut butter flavor is pervasive and, as the manufacturers of peanut M&M's and Reeses Pieces have so profitably discovered, it blends perfectly with the chocolate.

1/2 cup reduced-fat margarine (50% less fat)

1/2 cup reduced-fat peanut butter (25% less fat)

1 cup plus 1/3 cup sugar

1/2 cup dark brown sugar, packed

1 teaspoon baking soda

1/2 teaspoon salt

2 egg whites

1 1/2 teaspoons vanilla extract

2 cups flour

1/3 cup minichocolate chips

1. Preheat the oven to 350°F. Line a cookie sheet with parchment paper or coat with nonstick spray and set aside.

2. In a large bowl beat the margarine and peanut butter on medium speed until smooth. Add 1 cup sugar, the brown sugar, baking powder, baking soda, and salt and beat until smooth. Beat in the egg whites and vanilla extract. Gradually mix in the flour. Stir in minichocolate chips.

3. Shape the batter into balls using rounded ½ teaspoons to measure size and roll them in the remaining ⅓ cup sugar. Place on the prepared cookie sheet.

4. Bake for 12 minutes or until the edges are firm and the bottoms browned. (They will become crispy when cooled.) Allow to cool.

Makes 110 cookies

One cookie contains: 35 calories, 1.0g of fat

Chocolate Florentine Cookies

These thin, lacy, and crispy cookies are normally loaded with nuts. So, light and thin as they are, they are usually high in fat. Here oats have replaced the nuts. The crunch remains and the subtle chocolate taste is, if anything, even more pronounced than usual. And the combined flavors leave a particularly pleasant aftertaste.

1/2 cup Smart Beat margarine, melted

2 cups rolled oats

1 cup plus 2 tablespoons sugar

1/4 cup light corn syrup

1/4 cup low-fat chocolate milk

2 tablespoons flour

3 tablespoons unsweetened Dutch cocoa

1/4 teaspoon salt

1 1/2 teaspoons vanilla extract

1. Preheat the oven to 375°F. Line a cookie sheet with parchment paper or coat with nonstick spray and set aside.

2. In a medium bowl combine the margarine, oats, and sugar and blend well. Stir in the corn syrup, chocolate milk, flour, cocoa, salt, and vanilla extract and mix well.

3. Drop the batter by rounded ½ teaspoonfuls, about 2 inches apart, onto the prepared cookie sheet. Bake for 6 to 8 minutes or until golden brown. Cool completely on the cookie sheet.

Makes 85 cookies

One cookie contains: 24 calories, .4g of fat

Sweet Sesame Cookies

These flaxen disks are thin, crispy, and oozing with rich sesame flavor. The taste will be familiar to anyone who has eaten the sturdy sesame bars that are so prominently displayed near the cash registers of most delicatessens. These are far less rich than the candy and have a fresh-from-the-oven aroma.

2 tablespoons corn oil margarine

2 tablespoons Smart Beat margarine

1 1/2 cups light brown sugar, packed

1/4 cup orange-flavored honey

1 1/2 teaspoons vanilla extract

2 egg whites

1/2 cup sesame seeds

1 cup flour

1/4 teaspoon salt

1. Preheat the oven to 350°F. Line a cookie sheet with parchment paper or coat with nonstick spray and set aside.

2. In a large bowl cream the margarines, brown sugar, honey, and vanilla extract until light and fluffy. Mix in the egg whites, sesame seeds, flour, and salt until well blended. Place in the freezer until the dough becomes firm enough for easy handling (about 15 to 20 minutes).

3. Spoon the dough onto the prepared cookie sheet in rounded ½ teaspoonfuls about 2 inches apart. Bake for 10 to 12 minutes or until rich golden.

Makes 120 cookies

One cookie contains: 22 calories, .5g of fat

Vanilla Malt Cookies

Lighter than air, these tan wafers have a thin, cloudlike appearance. They are crunchy, with a distinctive vanilla malt flavor. The sparse sprinkling of chocolate chips produces, here and there, the occasional burst of chocolate flavor.

2 egg whites

1/8 teaspoon cream of tartar

1 1/4 cups powdered sugar

2 tablespoons Carnation malted milk

1/2 cup vanilla wafer crumbs (about 12 wafers)

1 tablespoon minichocolate chips

1. Preheat the oven to 375°F. Line a cookie sheet with parchment paper or coat with nonstick spray and set aside.

2. In a large bowl combine the egg whites, cream of tartar, sugar, malted milk, and vanilla wafer crumbs. With an electric mixer beat on high speed until the batter is thick and smooth. Place the batter in the feezer for 15 minutes.

3. Drop the batter onto the prepared cookie sheet by rounded ½ teaspoonfuls 3 inches apart. They spread out widely and the cookies become very thin and crispy. Sprinkle 4 minichocolate chips evenly over the top of each cookie and press them into the batter.

4. Bake for 9 to 11 minutes or until golden brown. Cool and store in an airtight container.

Makes 35 cookies

One cookie contains: 26 calories, .5g of fat

Poppy Seed Sugar Cookies

You will be surprised how much crunch and nutty flavor one tablespoon of poppy seeds can add to a batch of cookies. Although poppy seeds naturally contain a good deal of fat, so few of them are used in this recipe that they have virtually no effect on the cookie's fat content.

4 tablespoons (1/2 stick) corn oil margarine, softened

1 cup sugar

2 egg whites

1 teaspoon vanilla extract

1/2 teaspoon almond extract

1 1/3 cups plus 1 tablespoon flour

1 teaspoon cream of tartar

1/2 teaspoon baking soda

1/8 teaspoon salt

1 tablespoon poppy seeds

1/2 cup sugar for coating

1. Preheat the oven to 350°F. Line a cookie sheet with parchment paper or coat with nonstick spray and set aside.

2. In a large bowl cream the margarine and sugar until smooth. Add the egg whites, vanilla extract, and almond extract and mix well. Stir in the flour, cream of tartar, baking soda, and salt. Fold in the poppy seeds and set aside.

3. To coat, pour the ½ cup sugar into a small bowl. Spoon the dough by rounded ½ teaspoonfuls into the bowl of sugar and roll until coated.

4. Place onto the prepared cookie sheet 2 inches apart. Bake for 12 to 14 minutes or until light golden. Remove from heat and cool. They will become crispy when cooled.

Makes 90 cookies

One cookie contains: 25 calories, .6g of fat

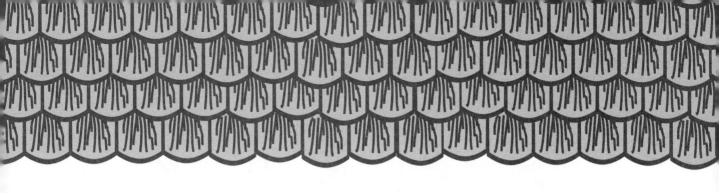

Brownies and Bars

A brownie is a cross between a cookie and a cake. It is denser and richer than a cake but not quite as dense as a cookie. The texture is rather fudgy and fillings are sometimes added. They are made in square or rectangular pans and cut into squares. Bars look like brownies but are usually denser and made in layers, so they can become more sophisticated, complex, and elegant.

Most of my recipes are extremely simple. They require, at most, one mixing bowl, but many are assembled directly in the baking pan. When covered in plastic wrap, all of these brownies and bars freeze perfectly and, when frozen, can last up to six months. As a general rule they have a longer shelf life than cookies or cakes and can be conveniently stored in their original baking pans.

The following are a few helpful tips for making brownies and bars:

- Use the size pan specified in the recipe. Changing the pan size changes the thickness of the bar and will affect baking time. The bars will get overbaked if the pan is too large and underbaked if it is too small.

- Cut the bars when the pan has cooled unless the recipe specifies differently. This will prevent the bars from crumbling.

Superfudgy Brownies

Every time I make this brownie for my kids and their friends they rave that it is the best brownie they have ever eaten. They don't even know it is low in fat. It is amazing how the slight amount of canola oil moisturized by the corn syrup and applesauce can make these brownies fudgy and gooey beyond all expectation.

2 egg whites

2 teaspoons canola oil

2 teaspoons vanilla extract

2 tablespoons corn syrup

1/4 cup plus 2 tablespoons unsweetened applesauce

1/2 cup plus 2 tablespoons sugar

1/2 cup dark brown sugar

2/3 cup flour

1/2 cup plus 3 tablespoons unsweetened
Dutch cocoa

1/2 teaspoon baking powder

1 tablespoon powdered sugar for topping

1. Preheat the oven to 350°F.

2. In a bowl combine the egg whites, canola oil, vanilla extract, corn syrup, and apple-sauce with a hand mixer. Add the sugars and mix. Add the flour, cocoa, and baking powder and mix until smooth.

3. Coat an 8 × 8-inch baking pan with nonstick spray and pour in the batter. Bake for approximately 18 to 20 minutes. (Incredible as it may seem, the key to this brownie is in the baking. It must be slightly underbaked to give it the superrich fudgy flavor and consistency. Bake it only until the outside of the brownie becomes firm. The inside must still be soft and slightly raw. Overbaking will change the brownie entirely by causing it to become dry and cakelike.)

4. Cool and cut the brownie into squares. Sprinkle the top with the powdered sugar.

Makes 16 brownies

One brownie contains: 103 calories, 1.1g of fat

Apricot Jewels

This recipe is simple to make and easy to clean up because you use cake mix as a base, there are only a handful of ingredients, and you do no mixing. But if you don't tell anybody you will get rave reviews anyway. I like Duncan Hines cake mix best, but Betty Crocker runs a close second and is a little lower in fat. The golden apricot preserves lend a sharp, fruity flavor to the heavy pastry base (Knotts is awfully good and has less than half the calories of regular preserves). The sweetened condensed skim milk imparts a sweet, creamy glaze to the fruit. In my old high-fat days I used sweetened condensed whole milk and nuts. Neither are necessary now and the recipe is still great.

1/4 cup Smart Beat margarine

1 1/4 cups yellow cake mix

3/4 cup light apricot preserves

1/2 cup rolled oats

1 1/2 tablespoons sugar and 1/2 tablespoon cinnamon, mixed

7 ounces (1/2 can) fat-free sweetened condensed milk

1. Preheat the oven to 350°F.

2. Put the Smart Beat margarine into an 8 × 8-inch pan and melt it in the oven. Sprinkle the cake mix evenly over the margarine in the pan and pat it down with the back of a fork or spoon. Spread the preserves over the cake mix. Sprinkle the oats evenly over the preserves.

3. Sprinkle the sugar and cinnamon mixture over the oats. Drizzle the condensed milk evenly over the top.

4. Bake for 30 to 40 minutes or until the top is quite brown. While it is still warm, cut it into 16 squares.

Makes 16 bars

One bar contains: 130 calories, 1.6g of fat

Chocolate Fudge Chewy

This is one of my favorite desserts because it has all my favorite ingredients from chocolate chips and oats to sweetened condensed skim milk. One can hardly go wrong. It's also simple to make and easy to clean up. I prefer Duncan Hines cake mix for this recipe.

1/3 cup Smart Beat margarine

2 cups Devil's food cake mix

3 tablespoons Hershey's chocolate syrup

1/3 cup semisweet minichocolate chips

1 cup rolled oats

1 can (14 ounces) fat-free sweetened condensed milk

1. Preheat the oven to 350°F.

2. In a 13 × 9-inch pan melt the margarine and spread it evenly over the bottom. Sprinkle the cake mix evenly over the margarine. Drizzle the chocolate syrup over the cake mix.

3. Scatter the chocolate chips and oats evenly over the cake mix. Drizzle the condensed milk evenly over the pan.

4. Bake for 35 to 40 minutes or until golden brown. Allow to cool 10 minutes in the pan. While it is still warm, cut into 30 squares.

Makes 30 bars

One bar contains: 97 calories, 1.5g of fat

Date-Oat Dreams

In its high-fat version this brownie used to be called a Date-Nut Dream. I have been able to dispense with the nuts, and you won't miss them because I have added oats. The mixture of golden dessert dates, oats, sugar, and Indian red cinnamon blend magically to produce this rich bronze, chewy bar. Because the base is a cake mix, this bar requires no mixing bowl. It can be assembled very quickly.

1/3 cup Smart Beat margarine

2 1/2 cups yellow cake mix

2 cups chopped dates

4 tablespoons sugar

1 teaspoon cinnamon

1 cup rolled oats

1 can (14 ounces) fat-free sweetened condensed milk

1. Preheat the oven to 350°F.

2. In a 13 × 9-inch pan melt the margarine and spread it evenly over the bottom. Sprinkle the cake mix evenly over the margarine. Spread the dates evenly over the cake mix.

3. In a small bowl stir together the sugar and cinnamon. Sprinkle the cinnamon/sugar mixture evenly over the dates. Spread the oats evenly over the cinnamon/sugar and drizzle the condensed milk evenly over everything.

4. Bake for 35 to 40 minutes or until the top is golden brown. Cool for 10 minutes and cut into squares while still warm.

Makes 30 bars

One bar contains: 138 calories, 1.7g of fat

Tip: These bars freeze beautifully in double plastic bags. Just remove them from the bag while defrosting.

Magic Cookie Bars

This is another old-time, classic bar that became popular in the early 1960s with the introduction of sweetened condensed milk to baking. And small wonder it was popular, full of butter, chocolate chips, graham cracker crumbs, coconut, and nuts. The penalty, of course, was that a small square contained 155 calories and 11 grams of fat.

My low-fat version of this gem of a bar maintains the scrumptious taste by substituting Cocoa Krispies and Smart Beat margarine for the nuts and butter while reducing the amounts of the other high-fat ingredients.

1/3 cup Smart Beat margarine

1 2/3 cups graham cracker crumbs

3/4 cup Cocoa Krispies

3 tablespoons fat-free hot fudge sauce

1/4 cup plus 1 tablespoon minichocolate chips

1/3 cup flaked coconut

1 can (14 ounces) fat-free sweetened condensed milk

1. Preheat the oven to 350°F.

2. In a 13 × 9-inch glass pan melt the margarine in the oven. Sprinkle the graham cracker crumbs over the margarine and using a rubber spatula, blend together. Press into the bottom of the pan. Sprinkle the Cocoa Krispies over the graham cracker crumbs. Drizzle the hot fudge sauce evenly over the Cocoa Krispies.

3. Sprinkle the minichocolate chips evenly over the hot fudge sauce. Spread the coconut evenly over the minichocolate chips. Drizzle the condensed milk over the entire pan.

4. Bake for 35 to 40 minutes or until browned. Cool 10 minutes and cut into squares while still warm.

Makes 30 bars

One bar contains: 80 calories, 1.7g of fat

Luscious Lemon Squares

The sharply acidic taste of fresh lemon juice is cut and softened by the rich, creamy sweetness of lemon cake mix and sweetened condensed milk to provide a tangy yet powerful lemon flavor. It is chewy and substantial. This lovely, golden yellow bar hints of warm summer afternoons but makes a great treat anytime.

1/3 cup Smart Beat margarine

2 1/2 cups lemon cake mix (not the pudding variety)

1 cup Rice Krispies

1 cup golden raisins

1 can (14 ounces) fat-free sweetened condensed milk

1 tablespoon lemon juice

1. Preheat the oven to 350°F.

2. In a 13 × 9-inch pan melt the margarine and spread it evenly over the bottom of the pan. Sprinkle the cake mix evenly over the margarine. Scatter the Rice Krispies and raisins evenly over the cake mix.

3. In a small bowl stir together the condensed milk and lemon juice. Drizzle the milk and lemon juice mixture evenly over the Rice Krispies.

4. Bake for 35 to 40 minutes or until the top is golden brown. Allow to cool for 5 minutes and cut into squares while still warm. Cut into 35 bars.

Makes 35 bars

One bar contains: 76 calories, 1.2g of fat

Zebra Fudge Brownies

Swirled stripes of dark chocolate and alabaster cream cheese give this brownie its "safari" look. But the taste is nothing like the African savannah; it exudes the heavy flavor of fudge augmented by ribbons of oozing, moist cream cheese. The cream cheese does not overpower the cocoa flavor but rather softens and richens it.

Filling:

3 ounces low-fat cream cheese

3 ounces fat-free cream cheese

1/4 cup sugar

1 teaspoon vanilla extract

2 egg whites

Brownies:

1 package (21.5 ounces) fudge brownie mix

1/3 cup water

1/3 cup unsweetened applesauce

2 egg whites

1. Preheat the oven to 350°F. Coat a 13 × 9-inch pan with nonstick spray and set aside.

2. To make filling: In a small bowl combine the cream cheeses, sugar, vanilla extract, and egg whites. Beat until smooth and set aside.

3. To make brownies: In a large bowl combine the brownie mix, water, applesauce, and egg whites. Beat for 1 minute with a spoon or hand mixer.

4. Spread half the brownie batter evenly over the bottom of the prepared pan. Spread the filling evenly over the brownie batter. Spoon the remaining brownie batter over the top of the filling. To marble, pull a knife through the batter in a curving motion. Turn the pan and repeat.

5. Bake for 30 to 35 minutes or just until set. Do not over bake. Cool completely. Refrigerate for at least 1 hour. Cut into squares.

Makes 36 brownies

One brownie contains: 86 calories, 2.4g of fat

Tip: Store the brownies covered in the refrigerator.

Robust Raspberry Bars

Deep red raspberry preserves are sandwiched between layers of a light, cookielike base and topping.

Crust and Topping:

4 tablespoons (1/2 stick) corn oil margarine

1 cup sugar

2 egg whites

1 teaspoon vanilla extract

1 1/3 cups plus 1 tablespoon flour

1 teaspoon cream of tartar

1/2 teaspoon baking soda

1/8 teaspoon salt

Filling:

1 cup light red raspberry preserves

3 tablespoons flour

1 tablespoon sugar

1. Preheat the oven to 350°F. Coat a 9-inch square pan with nonstick spray and set aside.

2. To make crust and topping: In a large bowl cream the margarine and sugar until smooth. Add the egg whites and vanilla extract and mix until smooth. Stir in the flour, cream of tartar, baking soda, and salt and beat until well mixed. Set aside ¾ cup of this mixture to be used for the topping of the bars. Press the remainder of the crust mixture into the bottom of the prepared pan and set aside.

3. To make filling: In a small bowl combine the raspberry preserves, flour, and sugar and mix until smooth. Pour the filling on top of the crust and spread evenly. Top with the reserved ¾ cup crust mixture one piece at a time, spreading the pieces evenly over the filling.

4. Bake for 25 to 30 minutes or until light golden. Cool for 20 minutes and cut into 20 squares.

Makes 20 bars

One bar contains: 117 calories, 2.4g of fat

Lighter-Than-Air Lemon Squares

This bar is a sandwich with a crust, a filling, and a topping. The crust is a delicate, buttery-tasting pastry. The filling is a light, sweet lemon custard, and the top is a potent lemon glaze. When you put it all together, the bar oozes with tempting lemon flavor.

Crust:

2 tablespoons corn oil margarine

1/2 cup sugar

1 egg white

1/2 teaspoon vanilla extract

1/2 cup plus 3 tablespoons flour

1/2 teaspoon cream of tartar

1/4 teaspoon baking soda

1/8 teaspoon salt

Filling:

2 egg whites

1 egg

1 cup sugar

2 tablespoons plus 2 teaspoons flour

1/2 teaspoon baking powder

2 1/2 tablespoons lemon juice

1 teaspoon grated lemon zest

Glaze:

1/2 cup powdered sugar

1 tablespoon lemon juice

1. Preheat the oven to 350°F. Spray an 8 × 8-inch pan with nonstick spray.

2. To make crust: In a medium bowl combine the margarine, sugar, egg white, and vanilla extract and mix until smooth.

3. Stir in the flour, cream of tartar, baking soda, and salt. With floured hands, press the mixture into the bottom of the pan.

4. Bake for 15 minutes. Set aside.

5. To make filling: In a medium bowl combine the egg whites, egg, sugar, flour, and baking powder. Blend well. Stir in the lemon juice and lemon zest. Pour the mixture over the warm crust.

6. Bake for an additional 30 minutes or until the top is golden brown. Set aside and cool slightly.

7. To make glaze: In a small bowl combine the powdered sugar and enough lemon juice for the desired spreading consistency. Mix until smooth. Drizzle over the cooled filling. Cut into squares.

Makes 16 bars

One bar contains: 133 calories, 1.8g of fat

Chocolate Peanut Butter Squares

It is hard to imagine anything more opulent than peanut butter and sweetened condensed milk mixed together. I use low-fat varieties of these ingredients to form the center of this bar, and the combination remains splendid. The batter that forms the top and base is dense and earthy, with the color of toasted oak. A sprinkling of minichocolate chips on top infuses a suitably subtle chocolate flavor.

Filling:

2 1/2 tablespoons reduced-fat peanut butter

1 ounce fat-free cream cheese

1 ounce low-fat cream cheese

1/4 cup plus 1 tablespoon powdered sugar

1/2 teaspoon vanilla extract

Brownies:

2 egg whites

2 teaspoons canola oil

2 teaspoons vanilla extract

2 tablespoons corn syrup

1/4 cup plus 2 tablespoons unsweetened applesauce

1/2 cup plus 2 tablespoons sugar

1/2 cup dark brown sugar

2/3 cup flour

1/2 cup plus 3 tablespoons unsweetened Dutch cocoa

1/2 teaspoon baking powder

Glaze:

1/4 cup powdered sugar

1 teaspoon reduced-fat peanut butter

1 teaspoon unsweetened Dutch cocoa

2 teaspoons light corn syrup

2 teaspoons nonfat milk

1. Preheat the oven to 350°F. Coat an 8 × 8-inch baking pan with nonstick spray and set aside.

2. To make filling: In a small bowl combine the peanut butter and cream cheeses and blend until smooth. Add the powdered sugar and vanilla extract and mix until combined. Set aside.

3. To make brownies: In a large bowl combine the egg whites, canola oil, vanilla extract, corn syrup, and applesauce with a hand mixer. Add the sugars and mix. Add the flour, cocoa, and baking powder and mix until smooth. Pour half the brownie batter into the prepared pan.

4. Spoon the prepared filling evenly over the brownie batter. Pour the remaining brownie batter over the filling. Swirl with a knife.

5. Bake for 23 to 27 minutes or until a toothpick inserted into the brownie 2 inches from the outer rim comes out clean. The middle will be set but a toothpick will not come out clean. You want the interior to be fudgy. Set aside to cool.

6. To make glaze: In a small bowl combine the powdered sugar, peanut butter, cocoa, corn syrup, and milk and blend until smooth. Drizzle the glaze evenly over the top of the cooled brownie. Cut into 16 squares.

Makes 16 brownies

One brownie contains: 165 calories, 2.2g of fat

Pumpkin Pie Bars

This bar is a new twist on the traditional Thanksgiving holiday favorite. While emitting hints of potent cinnamon and pumpkin flavors, this wholesome-tasting bar is less sweet and silky-textured than the pie. Its base is granola and oats so it is full bodied, hearty, and substantial.

Crust:

3/4 cup flour

3/4 cup granola (see Note)

1/2 cup graham cracker crumbs

1/3 cup plus 1 tablespoon Smart Beat margarine

Filling:

1 can (16 ounces) pumpkin

1 can (14 ounces) fat-free sweetened condensed milk

2 egg whites

1 egg

1 1/2 teaspoons pumpkin pie spice

1/2 teaspoon vanilla extract

Topping:

2 tablespoons graham cracker crumbs

1. Preheat the oven to 350°F.

2. To make crust: In a large bowl combine the flour, granola, graham cracker crumbs, and margarine and mix until blended and slightly crumbly. Set aside ½ cup of this mixture for use in the topping. Press the remainder of the mixture into the bottom of an ungreased 13 × 9-inch pan and set aside.

3. To make filling: In another large bowl combine the pumpkin, milk, egg whites, egg, pumpkin pie spice, and vanilla extract and blend until smooth. Pour the filling over the prepared crust. Sprinkle the remaining ½ cup crust mixture over the filling. Sprinkle the 2 tablespoons graham cracker crumbs over the crust mixture.

4. Bake for 35 minutes or until a knife inserted into the center comes out clean. Cool in the pan for 20 minutes. Cut into 24 squares.

Makes 24 bars

One bar contains: 95 calories, 1.2g of fat

Note: Choose a granola for which ½ cup contains 170 calories and 3 grams of fat.

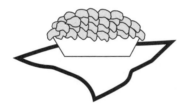

Oatmeal Toffee Blondies

This bar combines the seemingly incompatible elements of a sugary confection with the healthy earthiness of grain. Oats and brown sugar in the crumb topping convert the sturdy flavor of the oats into a delicious oatmeal breakfast bar.

Bottom Layer:

1 package (18.25 ounces) yellow cake mix

1/3 cup Smart Beat margarine

2 egg whites

Topping:

1 cup light brown sugar, packed

1 1/2 teaspoons vanilla extract

2 egg whites

1 egg

2 tablespoons flour

1 teaspoon baking powder

1/2 teaspoon salt

1 1/4 cups rolled oats

1. Preheat the oven to 350°F. Coat a 13 × 9-inch pan with nonstick spray and set aside.

2. To make bottom layer: In a large bowl combine the cake mix, margarine, and egg whites and mix at low speed until well blended. Press into the bottom of the prepared pan. Bake for 10 minutes.

3. To make topping: In a large bowl combine the brown sugar, vanilla extract, egg whites, and egg and mix until well blended. Add the flour, baking powder, and salt and mix well. Stir in the oats. Carefully spread the topping evenly over the warm bottom layer.

4. Bake for an additional 30 to 35 minutes or until golden brown. Cool and cut into squares.

Makes 36 bars

One bar contains: 102 calories, 1.9g of fat

Crispy Cocoa Bars

This is a fun bar that you can make with your kids and that the whole family will enjoy. You have seen this type of bar many times with loads of Rice Krispies imbedded in marshmallow. It requires no baking and just looks like it will be crunchy, sweet, and emit the flavor of the cereal. Here I have tinted the flavor with chocolate.

2 tablespoons Smart Beat margarine

2 tablespoons corn syrup

1 tablespoon sugar

2 tablespoons unsweetened Dutch cocoa

2 1/2 cups minimarshmallows

2 1/2 cups Cocoa Krispies

1. Coat an 8-inch square pan with nonstick spray and set aside.

2. In a medium saucepan over low heat melt together the margarine, corn syrup, and sugar. Stir in the cocoa and mix well. Add the minimarshmallows and cook over low heat, stirring constantly, until the minimarshmallows are melted and the mixture is well blended.

3. Remove from the heat and stir in the Cocoa Krispies. Working quickly, spoon the mixture into the prepared pan, press it evenly over the bottom of the pan, and allow to cool. Cut into squares.

Makes 16 bars

One bar contains: 60 calories, .4g of fat

Frosted Cool Breeze Brownies

This is an elegant and substantial substitute for the customary after-dinner mint. Frosty mint imbedded in gooey chocolate leaves your mouth cool and refreshed. And it gives the meal a sharp sense of closure. Unlike regular brownies, where you are often tempted to eat several, these mint-flavored goodies seem to satisfy one's dessert cravings with a single bar.

2 egg whites

2 teaspoons canola oil

2 teaspoons vanilla extract

1/4 teaspoon peppermint extract

2 tablespoons light corn syrup

1/4 cup plus 2 tablespoons unsweet-ened applesauce

1/2 cup plus 2 tablespoons sugar

1/2 cup dark brown sugar, packed

2/3 cup flour

1/2 cup plus 3 tablespoons unsweetened Dutch cocoa

1/2 teaspoon baking powder

Mint Frosting:

3/4 cup powdered sugar

1 tablespoon light corn syrup

1 tablespoon low-fat milk

1/8 teaspoon peppermint extract

1 drop green food coloring

1. Preheat the oven to 350°F. Coat an 8 × 8-inch baking pan with nonstick spray and set aside.

2. In a bowl combine the egg whites, canola oil, vanilla extract, peppermint extract, corn syrup, and applesauce with a hand mixer. Add the sugars and mix. Add the flour, cocoa, and baking powder and mix until smooth. Pour the batter into the prepared pan.

3. Bake the brownie for approximately 18 to 20 minutes. (As with the Superfudgy Brownie on page 94, the baking is key. The brownie must be slightly underbaked to give it the superrich fudgy flavor and consistency. Bake it only until the outside of the brownie becomes firm. The inside must still be soft and slightly raw. Overbaking will change the brownie entirely by causing it to become dry and cake-like.) Cool before adding frosting.

4. To make frosting: In a small bowl combine the powdered sugar, corn syrup, milk, peppermint extract, and green food coloring and mix until smooth. Cover the top of the brownie evenly with frosting and cut into 16 squares.

Makes 16 brownies

One brownie contains: 127 calories, 1.2g fat

Cherry-Vanilla Dream Bars

It will be hard to convince people that these sumptuous, creamy bars are not high in fat. The center is a smooth, off-white vanilla pudding, while the top is covered with succulent ruby cherries. And it all rests on a bed of deep brown graham crackers. It is like a cherry pudding pie and makes a wonderful, light dessert for a summer evening.

Crust:

1 1/2 cups graham cracker crumbs

1/4 cup sugar

3 tablespoons Smart Beat margarine

Filling:

1 can (14 ounces) fat-free sweet-ened condensed milk

1/2 cup water

1 package (3.4 ounces) instant vanilla pudding mix

1 3/4 cups fat-free frozen nondairy whipped topping, thawed

Topping:

1 can (21 ounces) cherry pie filling

2 tablespoons sugar

1 teaspoon vanilla extract

1. Preheat the oven to 350°F.

2. To make crust: In a medium bowl mix together the graham cracker crumbs, sugar, and margarine. Press into the bottom of a 13 × 9-inch glass pan. Bake for 8 minutes. Set aside to cool.

3. To make filling: In a large bowl combine the condensed milk and water. Mix well. Add the pudding mix and beat for 2 minutes. Refrigerate for 5 minutes. Fold in the whipped topping. Spread the mixture over the cooled crust. Refrigerate for about 1 hour or until the filling is firm.

4. To make topping: In a small bowl combine the cherry filling, sugar, and vanilla extract. Mix with a rubber spatula. Spoon the topping over the filling. Cover the entire pan with aluminum foil and refrigerate until time to serve. Cut into 20 squares.

Makes 20 bars

One bar contains: 156 calories, .7g of fat

Graham Cracker Custard Bars

Graham cracker is the dominant flavor in this unusual bar, augmented with nuances of vanilla and light chocolate. A thick, cool layer of moist custard adorns the firm, dark brownie base, and a sprinkling of chestnut-colored topping adds an attractive, sweet finish.

Crust:

1/4 cup Smart Beat margarine

2 tablespoons water

1/4 cup unsweetened Dutch cocoa

2 teaspoons vanilla extract

2 egg whites

2 cups graham cracker crumbs

1/2 cup powdered sugar

3 tablespoons sugar

Filling:

3 tablespoons Smart Beat margarine

1/4 cup low-fat milk

1/3 cup vanilla pudding and pie filling (not instant)

1 1/2 cups powdered sugar

Topping:

1 tablespoon graham cracker crumbs

1 tablespoon unsweetened Dutch cocoa

2 tablespoons sugar

1. Preheat the oven to 350°F. Coat an 8-inch square pan with nonstick spray and set aside.

2. To make crust: Place the margarine, water, and cocoa in a medium bowl. Heat for 30 to 40 seconds in a microwave oven until the margarine is melted. Mix together until blended. Add the vanilla extract and egg whites and mix well. Stir in the graham cracker crumbs, powdered sugar, and sugar and beat until smooth. Press the

mixture into the bottom of the prepared pan. Bake for 15 minutes, remove from the oven, and cool for about 15 minutes in the freezer.

3. To make filling: In a small saucepan melt the margarine over low heat. Blend in the milk and pudding. Cook about 2 minutes, until the mixture thickens slightly, stirring constantly. Remove from heat and beat in the powdered sugar with a hand mixer until smooth. Remove the crust from the freezer and spread the filling over it.

4. To make topping: In a small bowl combine the graham cracker crumbs, cocoa, and sugar and mix until blended. Sprinkle the topping evenly over the filling layer. Refrigerate for 20 to 30 minutes or until set. Cut into 16 squares. Store in the refrigerator.

Makes 16 bars

One bar contains: 147 calories, 2.2g of fat

Raspberry 'n' Cream Fudgy Brownies

Filling:

2 ounces fat-free cream cheese

2 ounces low-fat cream cheese

1/4 cup plus 1 tablespoon light raspberry preserves

1/2 tablespoon flour

1 egg white

2 drops red food coloring

Brownies:

2 egg whites

2 teaspoons canola oil

2 teaspoons vanilla extract

2 tablespoons corn syrup

1/4 cup plus 2 tablespoons unsweetened applesauce

1/2 cup plus 2 tablespoons sugar

1/2 cup dark brown sugar

2/3 cup flour

1/2 cup plus 3 tablespoons unsweetened Dutch cocoa

1/2 teaspoon baking powder

Glaze:

1/4 cup powdered sugar

1 1/2 tablespoons light raspberry preserves

1/2 tablespoon corn syrup

2 teaspoons nonfat milk

1. Preheat the oven to 350°F. Coat an 8-inch square pan with nonstick spray and set aside.

2. To make filling: In a small bowl combine the cream cheeses and preserves and mix until smooth. Add the flour, egg white, and food coloring, mix until well blended, and set aside.

3. To make brownies: In a large bowl combine the egg whites, canola oil, vanilla extract, corn syrup, and applesauce and mix until smooth. Add the sugar and brown sugar and mix well. Stir in the flour, cocoa, and baking powder and mix until smooth.

4. Pour half the brownie batter into the bottom of the pan. Spoon the filling evenly over the top. Pour the remaining brownie batter over the filling. Swirl with a knife.

5. Bake for 25 to 30 minutes or until a toothpick inserted 2 inches away from the side of the pan comes out clean. The middle should be set but still slightly fudgy. Cool.

6. To make glaze: In a small bowl combine the powdered sugar, preserves, corn syrup, and milk and blend until smooth. Drizzle the glaze over the cooled brownies. Cut into 16 squares.

Makes 16 brownies

One brownie contains: 135 calories, 1.7g of fat

Cinnamon Crispy Bars

This is another easy bar to make, cooked on the stove rather than baked in the oven, and a twist on the clasic Rice Krispie marshmallow bar. The pervading flaver is of sweet cinnamon.

2 tablespoons Smart Beat margarine

2 tablespoons corn syrup

1 tablespoon sugar

1/2 teaspoon cinnamon

2 1/2 cups minimarshmallows

2 1/2 cups Rice Krispies

Topping:

2 teaspoons sugar

1/2 teaspoon cinnamon

1. Coat an 8-inch square pan with nonstick spray and set aside.

2. In a medium saucepan over low heat melt together the margarine, corn syrup, sugar, and cinnamon, stirring until well combined. Over medium heat add the mini-marshmallows and stir constantly until the minimarshmallows are melted. Remove from the stove and stir in the Rice Krispies. Quickly pour into the prepared pan and pat it down.

3. To make topping: Combine the sugar and cinnamon in a small bowl and blend well. Sprinkle the topping evenly over the bars. Allow to cool and cut into squares.

Makes 16 bars

One bar contains: 58 calories, .3g of fat

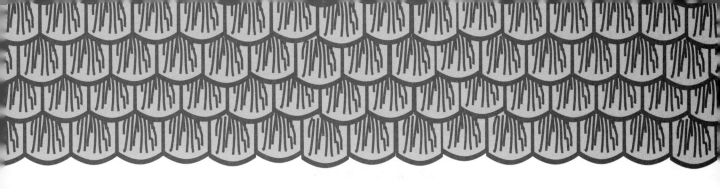

Cakes

In most cases low-fat cakes rely almost entirely on the frosting to carry the taste. Here they can stand on their own.

You will find these cakes to be very moist and rich tasting. And they vary in sophistication from simple snack cakes to elegant frosted layer cakes. Virtually all of them have some kind of frosting, glaze, or topping. They make the cakes look more appealing and add interest. The only negative to frostings and other toppings is that they contain a great deal of sugar and significantly increase the calories in the cake. Fortunately, I have been able to remove most of the fat.

Cakes rise because they employ leavening agents that create little air pockets throughout the batter. Most cakes can be divided into two categories depending on what creates the air pockets. One type uses baking powder or baking soda and the other uses egg whites beaten to create foam. The majority of cakes fall into the first category, while the second category includes angel food, chiffon, and sponge cakes.

The following are a few helpful tips for success in baking cakes:

- Use the proper size cake pan. If the pan is too large the cake will be thin, over-baked, and dry. If it is too small the cake will be underbaked and may have a sunken or sticky center.

- Always preheat the oven so that the baking time will be correct. Otherwise the cake will be underbaked.

- Measure ingredients accurately and add them in the order called for by the recipe.

- Cool the cake in the pan for at least ten minutes before removing. If it is removed too soon it may crack or break. If the cake appears to be sticking to the pan, return it to the oven for one minute and remove it from the pan immediately.

- Cut the cake with a thin, sharp knife.

- Check to see if the cake is done at the minimum baking time.

- Store the cake only when it is completely cooled. If the frostings or fillings contain dairy products, store the cakes in the refrigerator. If the cake is unfrosted you can store it in the freezer by wrapping it in heavy-duty aluminum foil. If the cake is in the egg white category, keep it in the pan when covering it with foil so it will not get crushed.

Carrot Bundt Cake with Cream Cheese Frosting

This moist, decadent cake is the perfect counter to the common fear that low-fat cakes are dry and tasteless. Fresh carrots and golden pineapple add a sweet, crunchy texture to the dense batter, and the cinnamon and vanilla give the cake its characteristic flavor. A thick layer of cream cheese frosting is the perfect topping for this substantial dessert.

7 egg whites

1 tablespoon canola oil

1 1/2 cups unsweetened applesauce

2 teaspoons vanilla extract

2 cups sugar

2 1/4 cups flour

2 teaspoons baking soda

1 1/2 teaspoons cinnamon

1/2 teaspoon salt

2 cups shredded carrots

1 can (8 ounces) unsweetened crushed pineapple, undrained

1/2 cup Grape-Nuts

1. Preheat the oven to 350°F. Coat a bundt pan with nonstick spray and set aside.

2. In a food processor or in a bowl with a hand mixer, combine the egg whites, canola oil, applesauce, and vanilla extract. Mix well. Add the sugar, flour, baking soda, cinnamon, and salt and mix well. Add the carrots, pineapple, and Grape-Nuts. Mix until blended.

3. Pour the batter into the prepared bundt pan. Bake for approximately 60 to 65 minutes or until a toothpick inserted into the center comes out clean. Allow to cool before removing from the pan.

4. Frost cooled cake with Cream Cheese Frosting (page 155).

Makes 12 servings

One serving contains: 336 calories, 2.4g of fat

Chocolate Fudge Cake with Chocolate Buttercream Frosting

Creating a heavy, moist chocolate fudge cake is the gold-standard test for a low-fat baker. It is a challenge because it is difficult to make the chocolate taste rich enough without adding fat. Here, a fine quality unsweetened Dutch cocoa makes a wonderful low-fat replacement for unsweetened chocolate, which contains cocoa butter. The evaporated milk and applesauce give this dark cake its moisture and density, yet in no way do they undermine the rich aroma of the chocolate. The result is a chocolate fudge cake that will satisfy the cravings of a true chocoholic.

1/2 cup low-fat chocolate milk

2 egg whites

1/4 cup unsweetened applesauce

1/2 teaspoon canola oil

1 teaspoon vanilla extract

1 cup sugar

1 cup flour

1/3 cup (1/2 of a 3.4-ounce package) instant chocolate pudding mix

1/4 cup unsweetened Dutch cocoa

1 1/2 teaspoons baking powder

1/4 teaspoon baking soda

1/2 teaspoon salt

1. Preheat the oven to 350°F. Coat a 9-inch cake pan with nonstick spray and set aside.

2. In a large bowl combine the chocolate milk, egg whites, applesauce, canola oil, and vanilla extract. Mix until blended. Add the sugar, flour, pudding mix, cocoa, baking powder, and salt and mix until thoroughly blended.

3. Pour the batter into the prepared cake pan. Bake for 35 to 40 minutes or until a toothpick inserted into the center comes out clean. Cool before removing from the pan.

4. Frost with Chocolate Buttercream Frosting (page 156).

Makes 8 servings

One serving contains: 312 calories, 2.3g of fat

Butterscotch Bundt Cake

Don't let the simplicity of this cake fool you. Its wonderful flavor comes from the pudding, while the buttermilk supplies creamy richness. The dusting of powdered sugar on top adds visual appeal and a final touch of sweetness.

4 egg whites

1 cup buttermilk

1/2 cup unsweetened applesauce

2 teaspoons vanilla extract

2 cups sugar

2 cups flour

1 tablespoon baking powder

1 teaspoon salt

1 package (3.4 ounces) instant butter-scotch pudding mix

2 tablespoons butterscotch chips

1 tablespoon powdered sugar for topping

1. Preheat the oven to 350°F. Coat a bundt pan with nonstick spray and set aside.

2. In a large bowl combine the egg whites, buttermilk, applesauce, and vanilla extract and mix well. Stir in the sugar and mix until smooth. Add the flour, baking powder, and salt and beat until well mixed. Stir in the pudding mix.

3. Pour half the batter into the prepared bundt pan. Sprinkle the butterscotch chips on top of the batter. Pour the remaining batter over the chips.

4. Bake for 50 to 60 minutes or until a toothpick inserted into the center comes out clean. Cool slightly and then remove from the pan. Dust the powdered sugar over the completely cooled cake.

Makes 12 servings

One serving contains: 262 calories, 1.1g of fat

Lemon Sunburst Layer Cake

This layer cake will be a surefire winner with everyone who sees and tastes it. The top is generously covered with a sweet lemon glaze that perfectly offsets a thick slab of tart lemon pudding separating the layers. The batter itself is fat-free but rich, moist, and incredibly flavorful because it contains lemon pudding, fresh lemon rind, and fresh lemon juice.

The look of the cake is perfect for spring or summer seasons. Elegant yet refreshing, the frosting is shimmering white with rays of yellow glaze radiating from its center like a holiday fireworks display.

4 egg whites

3/4 cup low-fat buttermilk

1/2 cup unsweetened applesauce

1/4 cup lemon juice

1 teaspoon grated lemon zest

1 teaspoon vanilla extract

2 cups sugar

2 cups flour

1 tablespoon baking powder

1 teaspoon salt

1 package (3.4 ounces) instant lemon pudding mix

Filling:

1/3 cup (1/2 of a 3.4-ounce package) instant lemon pudding mix

1 cup nonfat milk

Frosting:

2 cups powdered sugar

2 tablespoons lemon juice

1 tablespoon corn syrup

Yellow Glaze:

1/4 cup powdered sugar

1/2 tablespoon lemon juice

1/2 tablespoon corn syrup

1 drop yellow food coloring

1. Preheat the oven to 350°F. Coat a 9 × 3-inch round cake pan with nonstick spray and set aside.

2. In a large bowl combine the egg whites, buttermilk, applesauce, lemon juice, lemon rind, and vanilla extract. Add the sugar and mix until well blended. Add the flour, baking powder, and salt and beat until smooth. Stir in the pudding mix and mix thoroughly.

3. Pour the batter into the prepared pan. Bake for 60 to 70 minutes or until a toothpick inserted into the center comes out clean. Let cool for 15 minutes and carefully remove from the pan.

4. Place the cake in the freezer for at least 30 minutes or until firm and well chilled. When ready to serve, remove from the freezer, slice in half horizontally, and apply filling and frosting.

5. To make filling: In a small bowl combine the pudding mix and nonfat milk, mix with a wire whisk or mixer on low speed for 2 minutes, and set aside in refrigerator.

6. To make frosting: In a small bowl combine the powdered sugar, lemon juice, and corn syrup and mix on low speed until smooth and set aside.

7. To make yellow glaze: Combine the powdered sugar, lemon juice, corn syrup, and food coloring and mix until smooth and set aside.

8. To assemble the cake: Place one layer on a serving plate. Spread the filling over the bottom layer. Place the second layer of the cake over the filling. Spread the frosting over the top and sides of the cake. Drizzle the glaze over the top of the frosted cake.

Makes 12 servings

One serving contains: 366 calories, .5g of fat

Iced Banana Snack Cake

A snack cake is a small, single-layer cake that is usually faster to make than those with two or more layers. As always with fresh banana cakes, the most important secret to a wonderful, sweet, banana aroma is to use bananas that are overripe. Bananas, as a general rule, overpower the flavors of most other fruits. With low-fat cakes, lack of flavor is the primary obstacle that must be overcome in order to produce the kind of desserts that we all look forward to eating, and bananas solve this problem. Their potency makes banana cakes particularly tasty in their low-fat versions.

Here the cake batter itself is not too sweet, but it's fragrant with the familiar taste of the tropics. The velvety cream cheese icing brings the cake to life with a jolt of sweet, rich vanilla flavor.

1/3 cup Smart Beat margarine

3/4 cup sugar

3/4 to 1 cup mashed ripe bananas
    (about 2 ripe bananas)

1/4 cup low-fat buttermilk

1 teaspoon vanilla extract

2 egg whites

1 1/4 cups flour

1 teaspoon baking soda

1/2 teaspoon salt

1 teaspoon cinnamon

1. Preheat the oven to 350°F. Coat an 8-inch square pan with nonstick spray and set aside.

2. In a large bowl mix together the margarine and sugar. Add the bananas and mix until smooth. Stir in the buttermilk, vanilla extract, and egg whites. Add the flour, baking soda, salt, and cinnamon and beat until smooth.

3. Pour the batter into the prepared pan. Bake for 30 to 35 minutes or until a toothpick inserted into the center comes out clean.

4. Cool completely and frost with Cream Cheese Frosting (page 155).

Makes 10 servings

One serving contains: 219 calories, 2.5g of fat

Divine Mocha Layer Cake

The coffee flavor is intense. Mixed with heavy Dutch cocoa and sweetened with dark brown sugar, the coffee fuses into the most heavenly taste imaginable for a chocolate and coffee lover. The body of the cake is dense mahogany under a milk chocolate–colored frosting, bringing to mind the tropical South American plantations where the beans themselves originate.

2 egg whites

1/2 cup low-fat chocolate milk

1 tablespoon plus 1 teaspoon instant coffee

1/4 cup plus 1 tablespoon unsweetened applesauce

1/4 cup dark brown sugar, packed

3/4 cup sugar

1 teaspoon vanilla extract

1 cup flour

1/3 cup (1/2 of a 3.4-ounce package) instant chocolate pudding mix

1 1/2 teaspoons baking powder

1/2 teaspoon salt

1/4 cup unsweetened Dutch cocoa

1. Preheat the oven to 350°F. Coat a 9-inch round cake pan with nonstick spray and set aside.

2. In a large bowl combine the egg whites, chocolate milk, coffee, and applesauce. Stir in the brown sugar, sugar, and vanilla extract and mix until smooth. Add the flour, pudding mix, baking powder, salt, and cocoa and beat until smooth.

3. Pour the batter into the prepared pan. Bake for 35 to 40 minutes or until a toothpick inserted into the center comes out smooth.

4. Cool and frost with Chocolate Mocha Frosting (page 157).

Makes 8 servings

One serving contains: 314 calories, 1.3g of fat

Boysenberry Ribbon Coffee Cake

This rich cakelike bread is topped with a sweet, cinnamon crust, and a hint of fruity flavor emanates from its inner ribbon of boysenberry preserves. It is an ideal complement to breakfast or a family brunch.

4 egg whites

1/2 cup plus 2 tablespoons unsweetened applesauce

1 cup low-fat buttermilk

2 teaspoons vanilla extract

2 cups sugar

2 cups flour

1 tablespoon baking powder

1 teaspoon salt

1 package (3.4 ounces) instant vanilla pudding mix

1 cup light boysenberry preserves for filling

Topping:

1/3 cup flour

1/2 cup light brown sugar, packed

1/2 teaspoon cinnamon

1/4 cup rolled oats

3 tablespoons Smart Beat margarine

1. Preheat the oven to 350°F. Coat a 9 × 3-inch springform pan with nonstick spray and set aside.

2. In a large bowl combine the egg whites, applesauce, buttermilk, and vanilla extract. Stir in the sugar and blend well. Add the flour, baking powder, salt, and pudding mix and beat until smooth.

3. Spread half the batter into the prepared pan. Top the batter with the boysenberry preserves. Carefully spread the remaining batter over the preserves and set aside.

4. To make topping: In a medium bowl combine the flour, brown sugar, cinnamon, and oats. Using a pastry blender or fork add the margarine and mix until crumbly. Sprinkle the mixture over the cake batter.

5. Bake for 55 to 65 minutes or until deep golden brown. Cool for 10 minutes and remove from the pan.

Makes 12 servings

One serving contains: 342 calories, 1.1g of fat

Fruit Cocktail Snack Cake

This cake is so buttery tasting and moist that it seems almost incredible that it could be virtually fat-free. Although I liked canned fruit cocktail as a kid and my kids still like it, I am not normally a fan of this concoction where all the fruit tastes the same, not to mention being too soft and too sweet.

This cake was popular during World War II, when working women turned to canned goods more and more because they spent so much time outside the home. For years I put off trying this recipe because I was not attracted to the ingredients. But I was in for a wonderful surprise. Here the fruit cocktail provides just the right amount of moisture and, somehow, subtle hints of peach, pear, and pineapple tantalize your taste buds from bite to bite.

4 egg whites

1/3 cup evaporated skim milk

1 1/2 cups sugar

1 1/4 teaspoons salt

2 teaspoons baking soda

2 cups flour

1 can (16 ounces) fruit cocktail

Glaze:

3/4 cup sugar

1/3 cup evaporated skim milk

2 tablespoons Smart Beat margarine

1 teaspoon vanilla extract

1. Preheat the oven to 350°F. Coat a 13 × 9-inch cake pan with nonstick spray and set aside.

2. In a large bowl beat together the egg whites, milk, sugar, salt, baking soda, flour, and undrained fruit cocktail.

3. Pour the batter into the prepared pan. Bake for 30 minutes or until a toothpick inserted into the center comes out clean.

4. To make glaze: In a small bowl combine the sugar, milk, margarine, and vanilla extract. With a fork lightly poke the top of the cake about 25 times so that the glaze will seep into the cake. Disperse the holes evenly over the top of the cake. Pour the glaze over the cake.

Makes 24 servings

One serving contains: 129 calories, .3g of fat

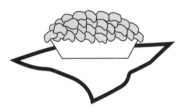

French Vanilla Layer Cake

This cake is the vanilla-lover's counterpart to the decadent chocolate fudge cake. This magnificent bundt cake makes a lovely ending for a dinner party. Vanilla itself has a clean and simple taste, and its enthusiasts can consume particularly large quantities of it without tiring of its flavor. As usual, the pudding added to the batter serves as an excellent source of moisture, flavor, and richness.

1 cup low-fat milk

4 egg whites

1/2 cup plus 1 tablespoon unsweetened applesauce

2 teaspoons canola oil

2 cups sugar

2 cups flour

1 package (3.4 ounces) instant French vanilla (or vanilla) pudding mix

1 tablespoon baking powder

1 teaspoon salt

2 teaspoons vanilla extract

Glaze:

1 cup powdered sugar

1 tablespoon corn syrup

1 tablespoon nonfat milk

1 1/2 teaspoons vanilla extract

1. Preheat the oven to 350°F. Coat a bundt pan with nonstick spray and set aside.

2. In a large bowl mix together the milk, egg whites, applesauce, and canola oil. Add the sugar and blend until smooth. Add the flour, pudding mix, baking powder, and salt and beat until smooth. Stir in the vanilla extract.

3. Pour the batter into the prepared bundt pan. Bake for 55 to 65 minutes or until a toothpick inserted into the center comes out clean. Cool in the pan for 10 minutes. Remove and cool completely before applying the glaze.

4. To make glaze: In a small bowl mix together the powdered sugar, corn syrup, milk, and vanilla extract. Blend until smooth. Drizzle the glaze over the cooled cake.

Makes 12 servings

One serving contains: 306 calories, 1.5g of fat

Chocolate Pudding Cake

This cake, oozing dark brown chocolate pudding, rekindles childhood memories. When you slice it you will see the glistening bed of chocolate pudding on the bottom. Make sure to spoon a generous dollop over the top of the cake. It is best served warm from the oven.

1 1/4 cups flour

1 3/4 cups sugar

6 tablespoons unsweetened Dutch cocoa

1 1/2 teaspoons baking powder

1/2 teaspoon plus 1/8 teaspoon salt

1/2 cup low-fat chocolate milk

2 tablespoons Smart Beat margarine, melted

1 teaspoon vanilla extract

1 1/3 cups water, heated but not boiling

1. Preheat the oven to 350°F.

2. In a medium bowl combine the flour, ¾ cup sugar, 3 tablespoons cocoa, baking powder, and ½ teaspoon salt. Stir in the chocolate milk, margarine, and vanilla extract, and mix well. Spread the batter in an ungreased 9-inch square pan. Set aside.

3. In a small bowl combine 1 cup sugar, 3 tablespoons cocoa, and ⅛ teaspoon salt, and mix well. Sprinkle the mixture evenly over the cake batter. Pour the heated water over the sugar mixture.

4. Bake for 35 to 40 minutes or until the center is set and firm to the touch. Serve warm.

Makes 12 servings

One serving contains: 177 calories, .9g of fat

Coca-Cola Cake

This cake was quite a rage during the 1950s and 1960s. Although the recipe is full of Coca-Cola, the cake itself tastes nothing like the beverage. It looks and tastes somewhat like German Chocolate cake: sweet, spongy, gooey, and delicious. On the other hand, it was the name that first tempted me to make the cake, and my kids were delighted with it because I rarely let them have Coca-Cola.

4 tablespoons reduced-fat margarine (50% less fat)

1/4 cup unsweetened Dutch cocoa

1 cup Coca-Cola

2 cups flour

2 cups sugar

1 teaspoon baking soda

1/2 cup low-fat buttermilk

1/2 cup unsweetened applesauce

4 egg whites

1/2 teaspoon vanilla extract

1 1/2 cups minimarshmallows

Cola Frosting:

1 tablespoon Smart Beat margarine

1/4 cup unsweetened Dutch cocoa

1/4 cup plus 2 tablespoons Coca-Cola

1 cup minimarshmallows

1 3/4 cups powdered sugar

1/2 teaspoon vanilla extract

1. Preheat the oven to 350°F. Coat a 13 × 9-inch cake pan with nonstick spray and set aside.

2. In a medium saucepan heat the margarine, cocoa, and Coca-Cola to boiling. Remove from the heat and add the flour, sugar, and baking soda and mix gently. Stir in the buttermilk, applesauce, egg whites, vanilla extract, and minimarshmallows.

3. Pour the batter into the prepared pan. Bake for 40 to 50 minutes or until a toothpick inserted into the center comes out clean.

4. To make frosting: In a medium saucepan heat the margarine, cocoa, and Coca-Cola until boiling. Reduce the heat and add the minimarshmallows, stirring until dissolved. Beat in the sugar and vanilla extract. Spread over the warm cake.

Makes 24 servings

One serving contains: 180 calories, 1.5g of fat

Cinnamon Swirl Coffee Cake

One of my great pleasures is to sit around the kitchen table with friends or family, sipping hot coffee, and nibbling on coffee cake as I repeatedly cut off additional slivers. (As you know, "slivers" of coffee cake have no calories!) This is a guaranteed winner of a coffee cake and great for coffee-time nibbling.

4 egg whites

1 cup low-fat buttermilk

1/2 cup plus 2 tablespoons unsweetened applesauce

2 teaspoons vanilla extract

1 cup sugar

1 cup dark brown sugar, packed

2 cups flour

1 tablespoon baking powder

2 teaspoons cinnamon

1 teaspoon salt

1 package (3.4 ounces) instant vanilla pudding mix

Filling and Topping:

1/2 cup sugar

3 tablespoons cinnamon

Streusel Topping:

1/2 cup powdered sugar

1/2 teaspoon vanilla extract

1 tablespoon low-fat milk

1. Preheat the oven to 350°F. Coat a 9 × 3-inch cake pan with nonstick spray and set aside.

2. In a large bowl combine the egg whites, buttermilk, applesauce, and vanilla extract and mix until blended. Stir in the sugar and brown sugar and mix well. Add the flour, baking powder, cinnamon, and salt and mix until smooth. Add the pudding mix and mix well. Pour half the batter into the prepared cake pan.

3. To make filling and topping: In a small bowl combine the sugar and cinnamon and mix well. Sprinkle half the prepared cinnamon/sugar mixture over the batter. Pour the remaining batter over the cinnamon/sugar mixture. Sprinkle the top with the remaining cinnamon/sugar mixture.

4. Bake for 65 to 70 minutes or until a toothpick inserted into the center comes out clean. Let the cake cool in the pan for at least 30 minutes.

5. To make streusel topping: In a small bowl combine the powdered sugar, vanilla extract, and milk and mix well. Drizzle over the top of the cooled cake.

Makes 12 servings

One serving contains: 311 calories, .5g of fat

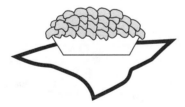

Almond-Glazed Angel Food Cake

Like meringues, angel food cakes have always been fat-free, light, and spongy. Unfortunately there is a flip side to these benefits, which is that angel food cakes tend to be bland by themselves. They need frostings or other additives to enhance their flavor and create interest. On more then one occasion, in fact, I have been suckered into buying plain, packaged angel food cakes by their appealing looks and nutritional information. With eager anticipation I settled down with a hefty slice and a cup of coffee, only to become totally disenchanted with the bland flavor in a few bites.

This version is snowy in color and boasts a feathery vanilla flavor with a hint of almond. The almond cream glaze adds great life to the cake.

1 1/2 cups sifted cake flour	1 1/2 teaspoons cream of tartar
2 cups sugar	1 1/2 teaspoons vanilla extract
1/2 teaspoon salt	1 teaspoon almond extract
1 1/2 cups egg whites (about 12 egg whites)	

Glaze:

2 cups powdered sugar	1 1/2 to 2 tablespoons low-fat milk
2 tablespoons corn syrup	1 teaspoon almond extract

1. Preheat the oven to 375°F. Coat a 10-inch tube pan with nonstick spray and set aside.

2. In a small bowl sift together the flour and 1 cup sugar 4 times.

3. In another small bowl sift the remaining cup of sugar alone 4 times.

4. In a large bowl beat the salt and egg whites with a hand mixer until foamy. Add the cream of tartar and beat until stiff. Add the sifted sugar, 2 tablespoons at a time, mixing at low speed. Stir in the vanilla and almond extracts. Gently but quickly fold in the sifted flour and sugar mixture, 2 tablespoons at a time. Be careful not to over-work the batter.

5. Pour the batter into the prepared pan. Bake for 30 minutes or until an inserted cake tester comes out clean. Immediately invert the cake onto a funnel or soft drink bottle and let it hang until completely cool.

6. Remove the cooled cake from the pan.

7. To make glaze: In a small bowl mix together the powdered sugar, corn syrup, milk, and almond extract until smooth. Spread evenly over the top and sides of the cooled cake.

Makes 12 servings

One serving contains: 201 calories, .2g of fat

Frosted Mocha Angel Food Cake

Fluffy and light in body with a hint of coffee and chocolate, this cake's flavors are subtle, and it is delicately sweet. The real power of the cake is in the mocha frosting. This milk chocolate–hued crown exudes the heady aroma of coffee and chocolate.

1 1/2 cups sifted cake flour

2 cups sugar

1/4 cup unsweetened Dutch cocoa

2 teaspoons instant coffee

1/2 teaspoon salt

1 1/2 cups egg whites (about 12 egg whites)

1 1/2 teaspoons cream of tartar

2 teaspoons vanilla extract

Frosting:

2 teaspoons instant coffee

1 teaspoon hot water

2 cups powdered sugar

1/4 cup unsweetened Dutch cocoa

2 tablespoons light corn syrup

3 to 4 tablespoons low-fat milk

1 teaspoon vanilla extract

1. Preheat the oven to 375°F. Coat a 10-inch angel food cake pan with nonstick spray and set aside.

2. In a small bowl sift together the flour and 1 cup sugar 4 times and set aside.

3. In another small bowl sift the remaining cup of sugar alone 4 times and set aside.

4. In a third small bowl sift together the cocoa and coffee and set aside.

5. In a large bowl combine the salt and egg whites and beat using a hand mixer until foamy. Add the cream of tartar and beat until stiff. Add the sifted sugar 2 table-spoons at a time, beating at low speed. Stir in the vanilla extract. Fold in the sifted flour and sugar 2 tablespoons at a time. Pour half the batter into the prepared pan.

6. To the remaining batter, gradually fold in the coffee and cocoa mixture and mix until well blended. Pour the mocha batter on top of the vanilla extract batter. With a knife or metal spatula cut through the batters for a marbled effect.

7. Bake for 30 to 35 minutes or until a toothpick inserted into the cake comes out clean. The top of the crust will be firm. Do not underbake the cake. Invert the pan on a funnel or bottle. Cool completely for at least 1½ hours.

8. Carefully run a knife along the side of the pan to loosen the cake and remove it from the pan. Place on a serving plate.

9. To make frosting: In a medium bowl dissolve the coffee in the hot water. Add the powdered sugar and cocoa and stir until well blended. Add the corn syrup and vanilla extract and stir until blended. Spread the frosting evenly over the cooled cake.

Makes 12 servings

One serving contains: 301 calories, .7g of fat

"No Time to Bake" Cakes

Most people seem terribly proud to declare that they bake only from scratch. Using cake mixes seems like cheating. So I guess that makes me a cheater because I like to keep a supply of cake mixes on hand for those occasions when I need a gourmet cake in a hurry. They can be assembled in minutes with the use of only one bowl, so minimal preparation and cleanup are required. In addition, with some creative effort they can be low in fat, exceptionally moist, and taste as good or better than most fattening scratch cakes.

It is also a good way to have a family project and introduce young children to baking. Scratch cakes are often too precise and complex for a young child's attention span and coordination. These cakes use only a handful of ingredients, are easy to measure, and are hard to mess up.

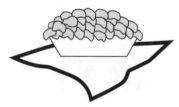

Cookies 'n' Cream Bundt Cake

Oreo cookie lovers rejoice. Now you can have your cookies and eat them too! This fascinating treat tastes like an enormous, light Oreo cookie in the form of a cake. And as a bonus it is simplicity itself to make.

1 package (18.25 ounces) French vanilla cake mix (White cake mix is okay if you can't find French vanilla.)

1 cup water

1/4 cup low-fat milk

1/3 cup unsweetened applesauce

3 egg whites

1 teaspoon vanilla extract

1 cup coarsely crushed reduced-fat Oreo cookies

1 tablespoon powdered sugar for topping

1. Preheat the oven to 350°F. Coat a bundt pan with nonstick spray and set aside.

2. In a large bowl combine the cake mix, water, milk, applesauce, egg whites, and vanilla extract. Beat for 2 minutes at high speed. Stir in the crushed cookies by hand.

3. Pour the batter into the prepared pan. Bake for 50 to 60 minutes or until a toothpick inserted into the cake comes out clean. Cool. Remove from the pan.

4. Before serving dust with the powdered sugar.

Makes 12 servings

One serving contains: 238 calories, 6.3g of fat

Lemon-Poppy Seed Bundt Cake

This scrumptious cake has only five ingredients, so it's quick to make (and even quicker to disappear). Like most desserts made from cake mixes and puddings, this cake is supermoist. The robust tang of fresh lemons and peel from the glaze add to the delicate crunch of the poppy seeds.

1 package (18.25 ounces) lemon cake mix with pudding included

1 cup water

1/3 cup unsweetened applesauce

1 tablespoon lemon juice

4 egg whites

2 tablespoons poppy seeds

Glaze:

1 cup powdered sugar

1 tablespoon lemon juice

1 tablespoon nonfat milk

2 to 3 drops yellow food coloring

1. Preheat the oven to 350°F. Coat a bundt pan with nonstick spray and set aside.

2. In a large bowl combine the cake mix, water, applesauce, lemon juice, egg whites, and poppy seeds and stir until moistened. Beat for 2 minutes at high speed.

3. Pour the batter into the prepared pan. Bake for 55 to 60 minutes or until a toothpick inserted into the cake comes out clean.

4. Cool for 10 minutes, remove from the pan, and set aside to cool completely.

5. To make glaze: In a small bowl combine the powdered sugar, lemon juice, milk, and food coloring. Blend until smooth. Drizzle the glaze over the top of the cake.

Makes 12 servings

One serving contains: 238 calories, 5.6g of fat

Cheese-Filled Bundt Cake

The cake is light and delicate, with a hint of apricot in the batter, sweet lemon-scented cream cheese filling, and a sugary lemon glaze. Although relatively simple to prepare, it appears complex because when you cut into it you find a thick white vein of cream cheese surrounded by yellow cake batter.

1 package (18.25 ounces) Duncan Hines yellow cake mix

3/4 cup apricot nectar

1/4 cup Smart Beat margarine, melted

5 egg whites

Filling:

4 ounces low-fat cream cheese

2 ounces fat-free cream cheese

3 tablespoons sugar

1 teaspoon lemon juice

Glaze:

1 cup powdered sugar

2 teaspoons lemon juice

2 teaspoons apricot nectar

1. Preheat the oven to 350°F. Coat a bundt pan with nonstick spray and set aside.

2. In a large bowl combine the cake mix, apricot nectar, margarine, and egg whites. Mix for 2 minutes or until smooth and set aside.

3. To make filling: In a small bowl combine the cream cheeses, sugar, and lemon juice and mix until smooth.

4. Pour half the batter into the prepared pan. Spoon all the filling evenly over the top. Pour the remaining batter over the filling.

5. Bake for 40 to 45 minutes or until a toothpick inserted into the center comes out clean. Cool and remove from the pan, then apply the glaze.

6. To make glaze: In a small bowl mix the sugar, lemon juice, and apricot nectar until smooth. Drizzle over the cake.

Makes 12 servings

One serving contains: 277 calories, 6.3g of fat

Blueberry Coffee Cake

I guarantee you will love this simple yet beautiful, delicious cake. It has a country look with a yellow interior, a scattering of deep purple blueberries, and a tangy, fruity apricot-pineapple topping. It fits well with a buffet brunch or afternoon tea.

Bottom Layer:

1 package (18.25 ounces) Duncan Hines yellow cake mix

1/2 cup Smart Beat margarine

4 egg whites

1/3 cup evaporated skim milk

1 teaspoon vanilla extract

1/2 teaspoon cinnamon

Filling:

3 cups fresh or frozen blueberries, thawed

2/3 cup sugar

2 tablespoons flour

1/2 teaspoon cinnamon

Topping:

1 cup light apricot-pineapple preserves (Knotts) or light apricot preserves

1 teaspoon lemon juice

1. Preheat the oven to 375°F. Coat a 13 × 9-inch cake pan with nonstick spray and set aside.

2. To make bottom layer: In a large bowl combine the cake mix and margarine. Cut the margarine into the cake mix using a hand mixer or pastry blender until coarse crumbs form. Add the egg whites, evaporated milk, vanilla extract, and cinnamon. Stir with a fork until smooth. Spread the batter into the bottom and 1 inch up the sides of the prepared pan.

3. To make filling: Sprinkle the blueberries over the prepared crust. In a medium bowl combine the sugar, flour, and cinnamon. Sprinkle this mixture over the blueberries.

4. Bake for 40 to 50 minutes or until golden.

5. To make topping: Warm the preserves and lemon juice in a microwave oven or small saucepan until mixed and easy to spread. Spread over the top of the warm cake.

6. Cool slightly before slicing. Cut into 24 squares.

Makes 24 servings

One serving contains: 151 calories, 2.7g of fat

Chocolate-Lemon Swirl Cake with Chocolate Glaze

I rarely see the combination of lemon and chocolate. That is a shame because the lightness of lemon complements the dark chocolate to produce a delightful taste. Slice this beauty open and expose the sharply contrasting colors of vibrant lemon and deep chocolate. A treat for the eye as well as the palate.

1 package (18.25 ounces) Duncan Hines lemon cake mix

1 package (3.4 ounces) instant lemon pudding mix

6 egg whites

1 egg

1 cup water

1/3 cup Smart Beat margarine, melted

2 tablespoons unsweetened Dutch cocoa

1 tablespoon sugar

Glaze:

2 cups powdered sugar

2 tablespoons Smart Beat margarine

1 teaspoon vanilla extract

2 1/2 tablespoons low-fat milk

3 1/2 tablespoons unsweetened Dutch cocoa

1. Preheat the oven to 350°F. Coat a bundt pan with nonstick spray and set aside.

2. In a large bowl combine the cake mix, pudding mix, egg whites, egg, water, and margarine to make the lemon batter. Beat at medium speed with an electric mixer for 2 minutes and set aside.

3. Place 1 cup of this batter into a small bowl. Stir in the cocoa and sugar to make the chocolate batter.

4. Pour the remaining lemon batter into the prepared pan. Spoon the chocolate batter on top of the lemon batter. Run a knife through the batter to marble it.

5. Bake for 50 to 55 minutes or until a toothpick inserted into the center comes out clean. Cool.

6. To make glaze: In a medium bowl combine the sugar, margarine, vanilla extract, milk, and cocoa and mix until smooth. Spoon evenly over the top of the cake and let it drizzle down the sides.

Makes 16 servings

One serving contains: 325 calories, 6.0g of fat

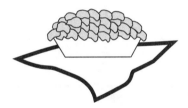

Golden Layered Creamy Peach Cake

Two layers of golden butter cake surrounded by ivory cream cheese and glistening amber peaches make this an elegant-looking cake and will elicit oohs and aahs as a grand finale to a special dinner party.

1 package (18.25 ounces) Duncan Hines Butter Recipe golden cake mix

4 egg whites

1 egg

1/4 cup plus 2 tablespoons unsweetened applesauce

2 tablespoons Smart Beat margarine

2/3 cup water

Frosting:

6 ounces low-fat cream cheese

6 ounces fat-free cream cheese

2/3 cup sugar

1 teaspoon vanilla extract

2 tablespoons low-fat milk

Topping:

1 can (21 ounces) peach pie filling

1 teaspoon cinnamon

1. Preheat the oven to 350°F. Coat two 9-inch round cake pans with nonstick spray and set aside.

2. In a large bowl blend the cake mix, egg whites, egg, applesauce, margarine, and water until moistened. Beat at medium speed for 2 minutes. Pour the mixture into the cake pans and bake for 30 to 35 minutes or until a toothpick inserted into the center comes out clean.

3. Cool the layers and then freeze for 1 hour so they can be more easily frosted.

4. To make frosting: In a medium bowl beat the cream cheeses, sugar, vanilla extract, and milk until smooth and set aside.

5. Remove the 2 cake layers from the freezer. Place one layer on a cake plate. Spread with ⅓ the prepared cream cheese frosting, and place the other cake layer on top. Frost the cake, both top and sides, with the remaining cream cheese frosting.

6. To make topping: In a small bowl combine the peach pie filling and cinnamon, and mix well. Spread evenly over the top of the frosted cake. Refrigerate until ready to serve.

Makes 16 servings

One serving contains: 266 calories, 5.1g of fat

White Almond Cake

Light and elegant, this snowy dream of a cake is the perfect ending to a festive evening.

1 package (18.25 ounces) Duncan Hines white cake mix

1 cup water

2 1/2 teaspoons almond extract

4 egg whites

1/3 cup unsweetened applesauce

1 teaspoon canola oil

Glaze:

1 cup powdered sugar

1/2 teaspoon almond extract

1 tablespoon corn syrup

2 tablespoons nonfat milk

1. Preheat the oven to 350°F. Coat a bundt pan with nonstick spray and set aside.

2. In a large bowl combine the cake mix, water, almond extract, egg whites, applesauce, and oil. Blend on low speed until smooth. Beat on high speed for 2 minutes until very smooth. Pour into the prepared pan.

3. Bake for 45 to 55 minutes or until a toothpick inserted into the center comes out clean. Cool the cake for 10 minutes and remove from the pan. Cool completely before applying glaze.

4. To make glaze: In a small bowl combine the powdered sugar, almond extract, corn syrup, and milk and mix until blended. Drizzle the glaze over the cooled cake.

Makes 12 servings

One serving contains: 235 calories, 4.4g of fat

Chocolate-Cherry Bundt Cake

Deep, dark chocolate batter embraces chunks of ruby-colored cherries in this romantic cake. The light crimson glaze adds a touch of blush to the top, and the overall flavor hints of chocolate-covered cherries.

1 package (18.25 ounces) Devil's
   food cake mix

3/4 cup water

1/4 cup unsweetened applesauce

2 teaspoons almond extract

4 egg whites

1 1/4 cups cherry pie filling

Glaze:

1 cup powdered sugar

1/2 teaspoon almond extract

1/2 tablespoon corn syrup

1/4 cup cherry pie filling

Drizzle:

3/4 cup powdered sugar

1/2 teaspoon nonfat milk

1. Preheat the oven to 350°F. Coat a bundt pan with nonstick spray and set aside.

2. In a large bowl combine the cake mix, water, applesauce, almond extract, and egg whites. Mix until smooth and beat for 2 minutes. Fold in the cherry pie filling.

3. Pour the batter into the prepared pan. Bake for 45 to 55 minutes or until a toothpick inserted into the cake comes out clean.

4. To make glaze: In a small bowl combine the powdered sugar, almond extract, corn syrup, and cherry pie filling and mix until smooth. Allow the cake to cool for at least 30 minutes and then coat evenly with the glaze.

5. To make drizzle: In a small bowl combine the powdered sugar and nonfat milk and blend well. Drizzle over the top of the cooled cake.

Makes 12 servings

One serving contains: 290 calories, 4.1g of fat

Applesauce 'n' Oats Snack Cake

I picture a blustery wind howling outside while your family gathers near a crackling fireplace sipping hot apple cider and enjoying this hearty, harvest-colored cake.

1 package (18.25 ounces) spice cake mix

4 egg whites

1/2 cup Smart Beat margarine

2 cups plus 2 tablespoons unsweetened applesauce

1 cup quick oats

1/2 cup light brown sugar, packed

1 teaspoon cinnamon

1. Preheat the oven to 350°F. Coat a 13 × 9-inch cake pan with nonstick spray and set aside.

2. In a large bowl combine the cake mix, egg whites, margarine, and 2 tablespoons of the applesauce. Beat at low speed with an electric mixer until blended.

3. Pour the batter into the prepared pan and bake for 15 minutes. Pour the remainder of the applesauce over the baked cake and set aside.

4. In a small bowl combine the oats and brown sugar and mix until crumbly. Sprinkle the oat and brown sugar mixture over the applesauce layer of the cake. Return to the oven and bake for an additional 10 minutes or until light brown. Cool and cut into squares.

Makes 24 servings

One serving contains: 139 calories, 2.9g of fat

Frostings, Sauces, and Glazes

Cream Cheese Frosting

The trick here is to mix the low-fat and fat-free cream cheeses. Blended with vanilla, this frosting contains the lowest amount of fat that allows it to still taste like a familiar old-fashioned cream cheese frosting. I have tried fat-free cream cheese alone and it just doesn't work.

2 ounces low-fat cream cheese

2 ounces fat-free cream cheese

1 to 2 tablespoons low-fat milk

1 cup powdered sugar

1 teaspoon vanilla extract

Cream together the cream cheeses and milk until smooth. Mix in the sugar and vanilla extract until smooth. If the mixture is too stiff, add 1 more tablespoon of low-fat milk.

Frosts one 9-inch cake

One recipe contains: 662 calories, 10.5g of fat

Chocolate Buttercream Frosting

It took me a long time to develop a chocolate frosting with the rich, creamy flavor my boys love. I use Smart Beat margarine because it's very low in fat and calories and works well for baking. I don't recommend any of today's fat-free margarines for baking. I tried them all, but the results ended up in the garbage disposal.

3 tablespoons Smart Beat margarine

4 tablespoons unsweetened Dutch cocoa

1 1/2 cups powdered sugar

1 teaspoon low-fat chocolate milk

1 teaspoon corn syrup

1/2 teaspoon vanilla extract

1. In a medium bowl cream the margarine with a hand mixer. Add the unsweetened cocoa and blend until smooth.

2. Add the sugar, chocolate milk, corn syrup, and vanilla extract and blend until the consistency is proper for spreading. (If it is too thick you can add a little more milk to thin it.)

Frosts one 9-inch cake

One recipe contains: 839 calories, 9.2g of fat

Chocolate Mocha Frosting

1/3 cup sugar

3 tablespoons unsweetened Dutch cocoa

3 tablespoons low-fat chocolate milk

1 1/2 tablespoons light corn syrup

1 cup powdered sugar

1 teaspoon vanilla extract

2 teaspoons instant coffee, dissolved in 1 teaspoon boiling water

1. Mix the sugar and cocoa in a medium saucepan. Stir in the milk and corn syrup.

2. Heat to boiling, stirring frequently. Boil for 3 minutes, stirring constantly. Remove from the heat.

3. Beat in the powdered sugar, vanilla extract, and instant coffee until smooth. Cool before frosting.

Frosts one 9-inch cake

One recipe contains: 856 calories, 3.3g of fat

Fudge Frosting

1/2 cup sugar

3 tablespoons unsweetened Dutch cocoa

3 to 4 tablespoons low-fat chocolate milk

2 tablespoons Smart Beat margarine

1 tablespoon light corn syrup

1/8 teaspoon salt

1 1/2 cups powdered sugar

1 teaspoon vanilla extract

1. In a medium saucepan mix the sugar and cocoa. Stir in the chocolate milk, margarine, corn syrup, and salt.

2. Heat to boiling, stirring frequently. Boil on low heat for 3 minutes, stirring occasionally. Cool.

3. Beat in the powdered sugar and vanilla extract until smooth.

Frosts one 9-inch cake

One recipe contains: 1,309 calories, 10.2g of fat

Caramel Frosting

1/3 cup Smart Beat margarine

1 cup dark brown sugar, packed

1/4 cup nonfat milk

2 cups powdered sugar

In a small bowl blend together the margarine, brown sugar, and milk. Add the powdered sugar and mix until smooth. If the spreading consistency is too stiff, add more nonfat milk, 1 teaspoon at a time.

Frosts two 9-inch cake layers

One recipe contains: 1,890 calories, 11.1g of fat

Chocolate Glaze

2 cups powdered sugar

2 tablespoons Smart Beat
   margarine

1 teaspoon vanilla extract

3 1/2 tablespoons unsweetened Dutch
   cocoa

2 1/2 tablespoons low-fat milk

In a medium bowl combine all the ingredients, adding milk gradually for desired glaze consistency, and mix until smooth.

Glazes one 9-inch cake

One recipe contains: 1,056 calories, 7.6g of fat

Vanilla Glaze

1/4 cup Smart Beat margarine

2 cups powdered sugar

1 1/2 teaspoons vanilla extract

2 to 4 tablespoons hot water

In a medium saucepan heat the margarine until melted. Stir in the powdered sugar and vanilla extract. Stir in the water 1 tablespoon at a time until smooth and the consistency is that of thick syrup.

Glazes one 9-inch cake

One recipe contains: 1,014 calories, 8.2g of fat

Honey Butter Spread

1/2 cup light corn oil margarine or
   I Can't Believe It's Not Butter,
   light

1 1/2 tablespoons honey

1 package Equal (or 2 teaspoons sugar)

In a small bowl combine all the ingredients and mix by hand until smooth. Pour into a butter crock and store in the refrigerator. You may need to blend again before serving.

Makes 29 servings

One serving (1 teaspoon) contains: 20 calories, 2.0g of fat

Cinnamon-Raisin Cream Cheese Spread

Full of sweet, plump raisins and cinnamon, this creamy spread tastes great on date-nut bread, zucchini bread, or a bagel. In fact, it can do wonders for a piece of toast as well. It will keep for about a week in the refrigerator.

3/4 cup fat-free cream cheese, softened

2 teaspoons sugar

1 package Equal

1 tablespoon chopped raisins

1 teaspoon cinnamon

1 teaspoon vanilla extract

Place all the ingredients in a small bowl. Blend until smooth. Pour into a butter crock or small serving bowl.

Makes 21 servings

One serving (2 teaspoons) contains: 12 calories, 0g of fat

Strawberry Cream Cheese Spread

3/4 cup fat-free cream cheese

2 teaspoons sugar

1/4 cup chopped fresh strawberries

1 package Equal (or 2 teaspoons sugar)

In a food processor or with a hand mixer blend the cream cheese, sugar, strawberries, and Equal until smooth. Pour into a butter crock.

Makes 48 servings

One serving (1 teaspoon) contains: 5 calories, 0g of fat

Cheesecakes

Cheesecakes are my richest and most decadent desserts. Making them low-fat means making them relatively low in fat, but they still have more fat and calories for their size than any other dessert in this book. A small slice of regular cheesecake contains approximately 400 calories and 25 grams of fat. This is nearly an entire meal's worth of calories and practically more than a day's allotment of fat! Pretty scary. A comparable slice of my average low-fat cheesecake contains less than 250 calories and 6 grams of fat. Still, you'll probably want to save these for special occasions. If you're like me, you want to eat dessert every day (and plenty of it). There are many alternatives in this book that will allow you to indulge and remain within reasonable bounds.

I have had to mix fat-free and low-fat cream cheeses to obtain the taste I want. I would have loved to use only nonfat cream cheese, and I tried over and over to create a recipe that would work. Unfortunately, it was impossible. The texture was acceptable, but the taste was not that of cheesecake; it was something else—not terrible, but not cheesecake either. If I used low-fat cream cheese instead of fat-free the taste was great but the fat content became unacceptably high. I compromised by mixing the two, using as little low-fat cream cheese as possible that would still allow me to maintain the wonderful creamy taste that I craved.

I have to admit to one other compromise. I added one whole egg to some recipes in addition to egg whites, which are all that I normally use. It served to bind the ingredients so that the texture became sufficiently firm as well as to top off the richness. Had I been able to use all light cream cheese, the whole egg would not have been necessary. But adding the whole egg allowed me to cut the amount of light cream cheese in half, so I think it's an acceptable trade-off!

Cheesecakes are generally made in three layers. The bottom or crust is usually made from some variety of cookie crumbs such as graham crackers, vanilla wafers, gingersnaps, chocolate wafers, or even Oreo cookies. This allows the cake tremendous versatility since a change of base can completely determine the flavor. The difference in my approach here has been to replace the butter with Smart Beat margarine (one tablespoon contains 2 grams of fat and 20 calories) and to use half the usual butter amount. I like it even better this way. Normally one bakes the cheesecake crust separately and later adds the filling for a second baking. Otherwise the crust becomes mushy. But with my drier crust I can bake the crust and center together without problem.

The middle or body contains the cream cheeses. The final layer is the topping, which can also dominate and change the taste of the cheesecake as a whole. The classic taste is a sweet, vanilla sour cream topping, but for a nice variety I like to add different fruits or to replace the vanilla with other flavorings.

Classic Vanilla Cheesecake

The color of purest ivory, this opulent and graceful dessert will fulfill your every expectation. It is the kind of treat you were sure you would have to give up when you decided to reduce your fat intake. The simple crust creates a flavorful base for the velvety smooth cream cheese filling.

Crust:

1 1/2 cups graham cracker crumbs	2 tablespoons Smart Beat margarine
2 tablespoons sugar	

Filling:

8 ounces fat-free cream cheese	4 egg whites
8 ounces low-fat cream cheese	1 whole egg
1/2 cup plus 1 tablespoon sugar	1 1/2 teaspoons vanilla extract

Topping:

1 cup low-fat sour cream

1 cup fat-free sour cream

1/4 cup sugar

1 teaspoon vanilla extract

1. To make crust: Coat a 9-inch pie pan or springform pan with nonstick spray. Combine the graham cracker crumbs, sugar, and margarine in a bowl with a hand mixer and press into the bottom of the pan. Set aside.

2. To make filling: Preheat the oven to 350°F. In a large bowl use a hand mixer and beat the cream cheeses together at high speed until blended. Add the sugar and beat until smooth. Add the egg whites, egg, and vanilla extract and beat until smooth. Pour into the crust.

3. Bake for 40 minutes or until the center is just firm to the touch. Cool in the pan or on a rack for 45 minutes.

4. To make topping: Preheat the oven to 450°F. In a medium bowl mix the sour creams, sugar, and vanilla extract until smooth. Spread the mixture gently and evenly over the top of the cooled cheese cake. Bake for 5 minutes. Cool completely on a rack.

5. Cover loosely. Chill in the refrigerator for at least 5 hours or, for best results, overnight.

Makes 12 servings

One serving contains: 257 calories, 7.3g of fat

Strawberry Cheesecake

This uses the crust and filling of the Classic Vanilla Cheesecake (page 166) as a base, but tastes substantially different because the fresh strawberries in the topping completely overpower the vanilla. It has a fruity flavor and is less formal, lighter in taste, and more reminiscent of summer than the classic version.

1 recipe Classic Vanilla Cheesecake (page 166) without topping

1 cup whole strawberries, green stems removed

1 1/2 teaspoons sugar

1 teaspoon orange zest

1 1/2 cups fresh strawberries, slivered

1. Prepare cheesecake crust and filling as described in the recipe for Classic Vanilla Cheesecake.

2. To make topping: In a blender process the cup of whole strawberries, sugar, and orange zest until smooth. Refrigerate the mixture until ready to serve.

3. To serve: Run a thin blade between the cheesecake and the pan. Carefully remove the cheesecake from the pan. Slice the cheesecake. Top each slice with several teaspoons of strawberry topping and slivered fresh strawberries.

Makes 12 servings

One serving contains: 262 calories, 7.3g of fat

Divine Cranberry Cream Cheese Torte

The elegant center of this potent dessert is beautifully set off by the sharp combination of sweet and tart flavors from the sugar and cranberries in the topping. It makes a wonderful finale for your Thanksgiving dinner, but you needn't wait. It's great anytime.

Crust:

3 tablespoons Smart Beat
    margarine

1 1/2 cups graham cracker crumbs

Filling:

3/4 cup canned cranberry sauce
    (whole berries)

1 teaspoon vanilla extract

8 ounces fat-free cream cheese

4 ounces low-fat cream cheese

Topping:

1/3 cup light brown sugar, packed

2 1/4 teaspoons cornstarch

1 3/4 cups canned cranberry sauce
    (whole berries)

1. To make crust: Coat a 9-inch pie pan or springform pan with nonstick spray. Combine the margarine and graham cracker crumbs in a bowl with a hand mixer and press into the bottom of the pan. Set aside.

2. To make filling: Blend together the cranberry sauce, vanilla extract, and cream cheeses with a hand mixer. Spread over the crust and set aside.

3. To make topping: Preheat the oven to 350°F. Combine the brown sugar, cornstarch, and cranberry sauce in a small bowl with your hand mixer. Spread this mixture evenly over the top of the torte.

4. Bake for 45 minutes. Cool completely on a rack.

5. Cover loosely. Chill in the refrigerator for at least 5 hours or, for best results, overnight.

Makes 12 servings

One serving contains: 233 calories, 3.5g of fat

Optional: Before serving sprinkle 1/4 cup Grape-Nuts on top and pipe light whipped cream around the outside circular edge.

Chocolate Chip Cheesecake

It is amazing how much difference adding a few chocolate chips to a vanilla-based cheesecake can make. People look forward to the burst of chocolate flavor that is released every time they bite into the small lumps of chocolate scattered throughout the cake. I use minichocolate chips because they spread out better than regular chips.

The cake itself is more delicate and creamier than my Classic Vanilla Cheesecake because I use sour cream in the filling and a vanilla wafer crust.

Crust:

1 cup vanilla wafer crumbs

2 tablespoons Smart Beat margarine

Filling:

8 ounces fat-free cream cheese

8 ounces low-fat cream cheese

3/4 cup sugar

1/2 cup light sour cream

1 teaspoon vanilla extract

6 egg whites

1/3 cup plus 1 tablespoon minichocolate chips

Topping:

1 cup light sour cream

1 cup fat-free sour cream

1/2 cup sugar

1 1/2 teaspoons lemon juice

1 1/2 teaspoons vanilla extract

1. To make crust: Coat a 9-inch pie pan or springform pan with nonstick spray. Combine the wafer crumbs and margarine in a bowl with a hand mixer and press into the bottom of the pan. Set aside.

2. To make filling: Preheat the oven to 325°F. In a large bowl beat together the cream cheeses with a hand mixer until they are smooth. Slowly add the sugar, beating until smooth. Add the sour cream, vanilla extract, and egg whites, beating them in well with the hand mixer. Fold in the minichocolate chips with the mixer on low speed.

3. Pour the filling into the crust. Bake for 40 minutes or until the center becomes just firm to the touch. Cool on a rack for 45 minutes.

4. To make topping: Preheat the oven to 475°F. In a small bowl combine the sour creams, sugar, lemon juice, and vanilla extract. Gently spoon the topping over the cooled cheesecake. Bake for 5 minutes.

5. Cool completely on a rack. Cover the cake loosely and refrigerate for at least 5 hours or, for best results, overnight.

Makes 16 servings

One serving contains: 210 calories, 7.2g of fat

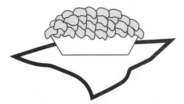

Apple Pie Cheesecake

This is probably the most elegant looking of all the cheesecakes. Each layer is distinctively colored and textured. The thick topping features golden apple peaks rising above a dark brown glaze of sweet cinnamon. And the off-white cream center perches upon a base of deep cocoa graham cracker crumbs. The taste is a spectacular confluence of apple pie and rich cheese cake.

Crust:

1 1/4 cups graham cracker crumbs

2 tablespoons Smart Beat
     margarine

1 tablespoon sugar

1/2 teaspoon cinnamon

Filling:

8 ounces low-fat cream cheese

8 ounces fat-free cream cheese

2 egg whites

1 egg

1 cup sugar

1/2 cup light sour cream

2 teaspoons vanilla extract

1 teaspoon lemon juice

Topping:

1 1/2 cups canned apple pie filling

2 tablespoons sugar

2 teaspoons cinnamon

1. To make crust: Preheat the oven to 350°F. Coat a 9-inch springform pan with non-stick spray.

2. In a medium bowl combine graham crackers, margarine, sugar, and cinnamon. Press into the bottom of the pan. Set aside.

3. To make filling: In a large bowl beat both cream cheeses until smooth. Mix in the egg whites, egg, and sugar. Mix in the sour cream, vanilla extract, and lemon juice. Pour the mixture over the crust and spread evenly.

4. Bake for 35 minutes or until the center is set. Cool completely. Refrigerate for at least 5 hours.

5. To make topping: In a small bowl combine the apple pie filling, sugar, and cinnamon using a rubber spatula. Mix to blend. Spread over the top of the cold filling. Store in the refrigerator until ready to serve.

Makes 12 servings

One serving contains: 233 calories, 6.5g of fat

Vanilla-Creme Cheesecake

This lush cake does not need a topping. It has only a filling and a base but both are unusual. The filling is particularly moist and rich because of the cream cheeses and sweetened condensed milk. Its flavor is predominantly vanilla but includes a trace of lemon.

The base has probably never appeared in a cookbook before because SnackWells vanilla creme sandwich cookies were only developed in the last couple of years— in the nick of time, I might add, to provide the perfect foundation for this luscious cake.

Crust:

1 1/4 cups SnackWells Vanilla
　　Creme Sandwich Cookie
　　crumbs (about 12 cookies)

1 tablespoon Smart Beat margarine

Filling:

8 ounces fat-free cream cheese

8 ounces low-fat cream cheese

7 ounces (1/2 can) fat-free sweet-
　　ened condensed milk

1/2 cup sugar

3 egg whites

1 egg

1/3 cup lemon juice

1 teaspoon vanilla extract

2 tablespoons all-purpose flour

1. To make crust: Preheat the oven to 350°F. Coat the bottom of a 9-inch springform pan with nonstick spray.

2. In a food processor or blender grind the cookies into crumbs. In medium-sized bowl add the cookie crumbs, less 2 tablespoons reserved for topping, and the margarine. Combine with a hand mixer. Press into the bottom of the pan. Set aside.

3. To make filling: In a large bowl beat both cream cheeses until smooth. Beat in condensed milk and sugar. Mix until smooth. Add the egg whites, egg, lemon juice, and vanilla extract. Mix well. On a low speed mix in the flour.

4. Pour into the prepared pan. Sprinkle the remaining 2 tablespoons of cookie crumbs over the top. Bake for 35 to 40 minutes or until the center is set.

5. Cool completely. Refrigerate for at least 5 hours.

Makes 12 servings

One serving contains: 207 calories, 5.4g of fat

Chocolate Cheesecake Squares

This is basically a cheesecake sandwich. Dense, dark, rich chocolate cheesecake is surrounded, top and bottom, by light vanilla and cocoa cookie crumbs.

Crust:

- 2 cups vanilla wafer crumbs (about 48 wafers)
- 1/4 cup plus 3 tablespoons unsweetened Dutch cocoa
- 1/4 cup plus 1 tablespoon powdered sugar
- 4 tablespoons Smart Beat margarine, melted

Filling:

- 8 ounces low-fat cream cheese
- 8 ounces fat-free cream cheese
- 1 cup sugar
- 1/4 cup plus 1 tablespoon unsweetened Dutch cocoa
- 3 egg whites
- 1 teaspoon vanilla extract

1. To make crust: Preheat the oven to 350°F. In a medium bowl mix together the vanilla wafer crumbs, cocoa, sugar, and margarine. Set aside ¾ cup for topping.

2. Press the remaining mixture into the bottom of a 9-inch square pan. Bake for 5 minutes. Cool and set aside.

3. To make filling: Reduce the oven temperature to 300°F. In a large bowl beat both cream cheeses until smooth. Gradually stir in the sugar and cocoa and beat until smooth. Beat in the egg whites. Add the vanilla extract and mix until smooth.

4. Pour into the prepared crust. Sprinkle the remaining ¾ cup topping over the filling. Bake for 55 minutes.

5. Remove from the oven and cool completely on a rack. Cover with plastic wrap or foil and store in the refrigerator for at least 4 hours. Cut into 16 squares before serving.

Makes 16 servings

One serving contains: 177 calories, 5.9g of fat

Rocky Road Cheesecake Decadence

Pillows of marshmallow and a sprinkling of dark chocolate chips decorate the top of this obscenely rich mocha-colored cake. I have deliberately designed it to be thin because its potency makes a small amount completely satisfying.

Crust:

1 cup Nabisco chocolate wafers, ground

3 tablespoons sugar

1 tablespoon reduced-fat margarine, 50% less fat (Fleischmann's), melted

Filling:

4 ounces low-fat cream cheese

4 ounces fat-free cream cheese

1/3 cup plus 1 tablespoon sugar

1/4 cup unsweetened Dutch cocoa

3 egg whites

1/2 cup light sour cream

1 teaspoon vanilla extract

1 cup minimarshmallows

Topping:

1/3 cup minimarshmallows

1 tablespoon semisweet minichocolate chips

1. To make crust: In a small bowl combine the wafer crumbs, sugar, and margarine. Press into the bottom of a 9-inch springform pan. Set aside.

2. To make filling: Preheat the oven to 350°F. In a large bowl beat the cream cheeses until smooth. Add the sugar and cocoa and mix until blended. Beat in the egg whites. Add the sour cream and vanilla extract and beat until smooth. Stir in 1 cup minimarshmallows. Pour into the prepared crust.

3. Sprinkle ⅓ cup minimarshmallows and minichocolate chips evenly over the filling. Bake about 20 minutes or until set. Cool on a rack and refrigerate for at least 3 hours.

Makes 12 servings

One serving contains: 154 calories, 4.8g of fat

Dreamy Apricot Cheesecake

Milky colored with flecks of golden apricot, the filling is a smooth mixture of sweet vanilla cream cheese and fruit. By itself it tastes much like a rich vanilla cheesecake with imbedded chunks of apricot. But the real punch of fruity apricot flavor comes from the apricot sauce, which is drizzled over the top of the individual portions immediately before serving.

Crust:

1 cup graham cracker crumbs

2 tablespoons sugar

2 1/2 tablespoons Smart Beat margarine

Filling:

8 ounces low-fat cream cheese

8 ounces fat-free cream cheese

1 cup sugar

1 1/2 teaspoons vanilla extract

2 egg whites

1 egg

2/3 cup light or reduced sugar apricot preserves

Topping:

1/2 cup light sour cream

1/2 cup fat-free sour cream

2 1/2 tablespoons sugar

1 teaspoon vanilla extract

Sauce:

4 tablespoons sugar

1/2 tablespoon cornstarch

1 teaspoon lemon juice

1/2 cup orange juice

1/2 teaspoon vanilla extract

1 tablespoon light apricot preserves

1. To make crust: In a small bowl combine the graham cracker crumbs, sugar, and margarine until well mixed. Press into the bottom of a 9-inch springform pan and chill.

2. To make filling: Preheat the oven to 325°F. In a large bowl beat the cream cheeses until smooth. Add the sugar and vanilla extract and mix until smooth. Beat in the egg whites and egg. Pour half this mixture into the prepared crust. Spoon the apricot preserves over the top. (If the preserves are too thick to spread, place them in the microwave oven for 10 to 15 seconds for better spreading consistency.) Pour the remaining cream cheese mixture on top. Swirl a little with a knife. Bake for 50 minutes or until set. Remove from the oven and set aside.

3. To make topping: Preheat the oven to 350°F. In a small bowl mix together the sour creams, sugar, and vanilla extract. Spread over the cheesecake. Bake for 10 minutes. Cool and then refrigerate for at least 4 hours before serving.

4. To make sauce: In a small saucepan over low heat stir and cook the sugar, cornstarch, lemon juice, and orange juice. Cook until thick and clear. Stir in the vanilla extract and apricot preserves. Top each slice of cheesecake with sauce before serving. Store the leftover sauce covered in the refrigerator.

Makes 12 servings

One serving contains: 241 calories, 5.9g of fat

Maraschino Cherry Cheesecake

Brilliant scarlet adorns the top of this cheerful cake. Its flavor is creamy, fruity, and infused with almond.

Crust:

3 tablespoons Smart Beat margarine, melted

1 1/2 cups vanilla wafer crumbs

Filling:

4 ounces low-fat cream cheese

4 ounces fat-free cream cheese

1 can (14 ounces) fat-free sweetened condensed milk

1/4 cup lemon juice

1 teaspoon vanilla extract

1/2 teaspoon almond extract

Topping:

1 can (21 ounces) cherry pie filling

Light whipped cream or fat-free frozen nondairy whipped topping (optional)

1. To make crust: Preheat the oven to 350°F. Coat a 9-inch springform pan with non-stick spray and set aside.

2. In a small bowl combine the margarine and wafer crumbs and blend well. Press into the bottom of the prepared pan. Bake for 5 minutes and set aside to cool.

3. To make filling: In a medium bowl beat the cream cheeses until smooth. Gradually beat in the condensed milk, lemon juice, vanilla extract, and almond extract. Continue beating until blended. Pour the mixture onto the prepared crust. Refrigerate for 4 hours or until set.

4. Spread the cherry pie filling evenly over the cold pie. Garnish each slice with light whipped cream if desired. Refrigerate leftovers immediately.

Makes 12 servings

One serving contains: 234 calories, 4.8g of fat

Pumpkin Pie Cheesecake

This cheesecake is different because the combination of tastes is out of context. The pumpkin pie flavor is familiar, yet in a creamy cheesecake it surprises the palate. Once you recover from taste shock, you will find it to be delicious.

Crust:

1 cup graham cracker crumbs

2 tablespoons Smart Beat margarine

2 tablespoons light brown sugar, packed

1/2 teaspoon cinnamon

Filling:

6 ounces low-fat cream cheese

3/4 cup light brown sugar, packed

1 1/2 teaspoons cinnamon

1/4 teaspoon ground ginger

1/4 teaspoon salt

4 egg whites

1 cup canned pumpkin

1 cup light sour cream

1 teaspoon vanilla extract

1. To make crust: In a small bowl combine the graham cracker crumbs, margarine, brown sugar, and cinnamon and mix well. Press the mixture into the bottom of a 9-inch springform pan. Set aside.

2. To make filling: Preheat the oven to 375°F. In a large bowl combine the cream cheese, brown sugar, cinnamon, ginger, and salt and blend until creamy. Add the egg whites and mix well. Stir in the pumpkin, sour cream, and vanilla extract, mixing until smooth and blended.

3. Pour the filling into the prepared crust. Bake for 45 to 50 minutes or until the tip of a knife inserted into the center comes out clean.

Makes 12 servings

One serving contains: 161 calories, 5.9g of fat

Banana Cheesecake with Strawberry Topping

Real dyed-in-the-wool banana lovers would enjoy this cake without the topping because the banana flavor is so dominant. But normal mortals will prefer it with the fresh strawberries and strawberry sauce because it cuts the powerful banana flavor while adding texture, tartness, and festive color.

Crust:

1/2 cup graham cracker crumbs

1/2 cup vanilla wafer crumbs

1 tablespoon sugar

2 tablespoons Smart Beat margarine

Filling:

8 ounces low-fat cream cheese

8 ounces fat-free cream cheese

3/4 cup sugar

1 1/2 teaspoons vanilla extract

2 teaspoons lemon juice

3 egg whites

1 egg

1/2 cup light sour cream

1/2 cup frozen nondairy whipped topping, thawed

3 large ripe bananas, mashed

Topping:

2 cups fresh strawberries, chopped

2 teaspoons sugar

1 teaspoon grated orange zest

1. To make crust: Preheat the oven to 350°F. In a small bowl mix together the graham cracker crumbs, vanilla wafer crumbs, sugar, and margarine and blend well. Press into the bottom of a 9-inch springform pan. Bake for 4 minutes. Cool and set aside.

2. To make filling: In a large bowl beat together both cream cheeses and the sugar until smooth. Add the vanilla extract and lemon juice. Beat in the egg whites and egg. Stir in the sour cream and whipped topping. Fold in the mashed bananas. Pour into the pie pan. Bake for 55 minutes or until set. Cool, then refrigerate for at least 5 hours.

3. To make topping: Set aside 1 cup of chopped strawberries. In a blender combine the remaining cup of strawberries, the sugar, and the orange zest and process until smooth. Refrigerate until ready to serve with the cheesecake.

4. To serve: Top each slice of cheesecake with 1 teaspoon of fresh chopped strawberries and 1 teaspoon of the prepared strawberry puree.

Makes 12 servings

One serving contains: 213 calories, 6.8g of fat

Pralines 'n' Cream Cheesecake

This cake, the color of burnt almond, has the look of flan or crème caramel in cake form. The various golden hues entice you to slice into it. And you will be rewarded by a sweet cake of supreme richness that tastes like a union of caramel and cream cheese. A small amount of it is quite satisfying. (One serving of a regular version of this cheesecake contains 380 calories and 29 grams of fat!)

Crust:

2 tablespoons Smart Beat margarine

1 cup graham cracker crumbs

Filling:

8 ounces low-fat cream cheese

8 ounces fat-free cream cheese

3/4 cup dark brown sugar, firmly packed

3 egg whites

1 egg

1 cup fat-free sweetened condensed milk

2 teaspoons vanilla extract

Top Layer:

1/2 cup dark brown sugar, firmly packed

2 tablespoons Smart Beat margarine

1. To make crust: Preheat the oven to 450°F. In a small bowl combine the margarine and graham cracker crumbs. Press firmly into the bottom of an ungreased 9-inch springform pan. Set aside.

2. To make filling: In a large bowl beat both cream cheeses at medium speed until smooth and creamy. Beat in the brown sugar. Add the egg whites and egg and mix at low speed until blended. Add the condensed milk and vanilla extract and mix until smooth. Pour on top of the prepared crust.

3. Bake at 450°F for 10 minutes. Then reduce the oven temperature to 250°F and bake for an additional 65 to 70 minutes or until the center is set. Remove from the oven and cool completely.

4. To make topping: In a small saucepan combine the brown sugar and margarine. Cook over medium heat until well blended, stirring constantly. Spread evenly over the cooled cheesecake. Refrigerate for at least 5 hours before serving.

Makes 12 servings

One serving contains: 259 calories, 4.9g of fat

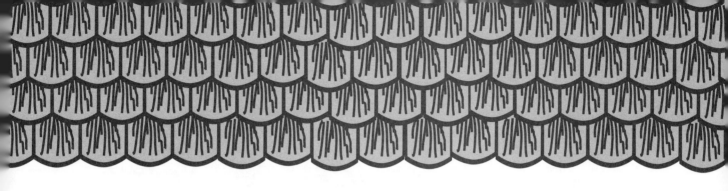

Pies

Many popular pies are naturally low in fat, particularly the fruit pies. The problems generally lie in the crust. Normal pie crust is loaded with fat, being composed primarily of flour and butter. I circumvent this by making my crusts from low-fat cookie crumbs and cereals. As with my cheesecakes, I use graham crackers and low-fat Oreo cookies, but in addition I use cereals, like Rice Krispies, and fat-free granola. In this way the pies are not only lower in fat, but easier to make, since mixing, rolling out, and forming a normal crust is the part of making a pie that I have always dreaded most.

Although these pies are easy to make, they will still turn you into a hero with your family and friends. They look great and are perhaps the quintessential American dessert, hence the expression "American as apple pie." People look forward to them at the end of a substantial meal because they are light and refreshing, unlike many heavy pastries. For an additional treat you can top your pie with light or fat-free whipped cream or make it pie à la mode with nonfat yogurt.

Fresh Strawberry Pie

Few desserts are as appealing to the eye as a glistening red strawberry pie. The berries themselves are only 55 calories per cup and are loaded with fiber and vitamin C. In fact the only potential shortfall of fresh strawberries is that they are sometimes disappointingly tart. With strawberry pie the sweetness of the glaze ensures that the berries will end up perfectly succulent and sweet.

Crust:

1 1/4 cups crushed graham
cracker crumbs

2 tablespoons sugar

3 tablespoons Smart Beat
margarine

Filling:

3 pints (6 cups) fresh strawberries,
hulled, washed, and drained

1 jar (18 ounces) glaze for strawberries
(You can find this product in the
produce section.)

Light whipped cream (optional)

1. Preheat the oven to 375°F. Coat a 9-inch pie pan with nonstick spray.

2. To make crust: Combine the graham crackers, sugar, and margarine in a bowl with a hand mixer. Press the mixture into the bottom and slightly up the sides of the pie pan. Bake the crust for 8 to 10 minutes or until golden. Remove from the oven and allow to cool.

3. In a large bowl combine the whole strawberries and the jar of glaze so that the strawberries are well coated. Pour the strawberry mixture into the prepared crust. Refrigerate for at least 3 hours or until set. When you serve, top with light whipped cream, if desired.

Makes 8 servings

One serving contains: 184 calories, 2.4g of fat

Pumpkin Pie

When the leaves start to fall in October and I see fresh pumpkins appearing every-where, I get the irresistible urge to make this pie. The filling differs from normal pumpkin pie filling only in the substitution of egg whites for whole eggs and skim milk for whole milk and tastes just as good. The real savings come in the crust where most of the fat usually resides. Reduced-fat margarine yields tremendous savings in fat content.

Crust:

1 1/2 cups graham cracker crumbs

2 tablespoons Smart Beat margarine

1 tablespoon plus 1 teaspoon sugar

Filling:

1 can (15 ounces) pumpkin

3 egg whites

1 can (12 ounces) evaporated skim milk

3/4 cup sugar

1 teaspoon cinnamon

1 teaspoon vanilla extract

1 teaspoon pumpkin pie spice

1 tablespoon cornstarch

1. Preheat the oven to 350°F. Coat a 9-inch springform pan with nonstick spray.

2. To make crust: In a medium bowl mix together the graham cracker crumbs, margarine, and sugar and press into the bottom of the pan.

3. To make filling: In a large bowl mix together the pumpkin, egg whites, evaporated milk, sugar, cinnamon, vanilla extract, pumpkin pie spice, and cornstarch. Pour this mixture into the prepared crust.

4. Bake the pie for 10 minutes. Turn down the heat to 300°F and bake the pie for an additional 35 minutes. Remove the pie from the oven and allow it to cool before serving.

Makes 10 servings

One serving contains: 107 calories, 1.8g of fat

Apple Cobbler

This is one of my very easiest desserts to make. Just open a can of apple pie filling, add some cinnamon and sugar, and put on the simple topping. Pop it in the oven and the incredible aroma of apple, cinnamon, and baking pie crust will fill your house. Baked and served in individual custard cups, it tastes and looks great, and you will get tremendous credit for your baking prowess with a minimal time investment. In fact the amount of preparation time is not an accurate measure at all of the attractiveness of any dessert.

Crust and Topping:

1 1/4 cups graham cracker crumbs

2 tablespoons Smart Beat
   margarine, melted

1 tablespoon cinnamon

2 teaspoons sugar

Filling:

1 can (21 ounces) apple pie filling

1 1/2 tablespoons sugar

2 teaspoons cinnamon

1. Preheat the oven to 350°F.

2. To make crust: In a medium bowl mix the graham cracker crumbs, margarine, cinnamon, and sugar and set aside.

3. To make filling: In a medium bowl gently mix together the apple pie filling, sugar, and cinnamon with a rubber spatula and set aside.

4. Spoon 2 tablespoons of crust mixture into the bottom of each of 8 custard cups. Spoon ¼ cup of the filling mixture over each crust. Sprinkle 1 tablespoon of the remaining crust mixture over the filling.

5. Bake for 10 minutes or until brown.

Makes 8 servings

One serving contains: 160 calories, 2.0g of fat

Cherry Cobbler

Simplicity and great taste are the hallmarks of this dessert. And baking it in single-serving custard cups provides a charming look along with a psychological benefit. People feel special because they get their own individual dessert. And all of us have a tendency to overindulge when there is more communal pie sitting in the center of the table. The hand automatically reaches out for that second slice, especially if there is still coffee left in your cup and good conversation to be had around the dinner table. Individual servings provide comfortable boundaries and a feeling of being finished when the dish is empty.

Crust and Topping:

1 1/4 cups vanilla wafer crumbs
(about 25 wafers)

2 tablespoons Smart Beat
margarine, melted

2 teaspoons sugar

Filling:

1 can (21 ounces) cherry pie filling

1 1/2 tablespoons sugar

1 teaspoon vanilla extract

1/4 teaspoon almond extract

1. Preheat the oven to 350°F.

2. To make crust: In a medium bowl mix the vanilla wafer crumbs, margarine, and sugar and set aside.

3. To make filling: In a medium bowl mix the cherry pie filling, sugar, vanilla extract, and almond extract and set aside.

4. Spoon 2 tablespoons of crust mixture into the bottom of each of 8 custard cups. Spoon ¼ cup of the filling mixture over each crust. Sprinkle 1 tablespoon of the remaining crust mixture over the filling.

5. Bake for 10 minutes or until brown.

Makes 8 servings

One serving contains: 157 calories, 3.4g of fat

Fresh Fruit Trifle

This dessert appears complex because it has several layers of cake, pudding, and various types of fruit. But it is simple to make because each ingredient is store-bought, and all you have to do is assemble it. When finished, this scrumptious trifle looks magnificent with its creams and fruits of many colors.

1 fat-free pound cake (10- to 12-ounce loaf, store-bought)

1/2 cup light strawberry preserves, warmed in a microwave oven for easier drizzling

2 containers (3.5 ounces each) ready-made fat-free vanilla pudding

1 cup fresh strawberries, sliced

3 kiwifruit, peeled and chopped

1 3/4 cups fat-free frozen nondairy whipped topping, thawed

1. Cut the pound cake in half horizontally and then into ¾-inch pieces.

2. Place half the cake pieces into a 2-quart glass serving bowl. Drizzle half the preserves over the cake pieces. Spread 1 container of pudding over the preserves. Sprinkle half the strawberries and kiwifruit over the pudding. Spread half of the whipped topping evenly over the fruit.

3. Repeat this sequence with a second layer.

4. Cover and refrigerate for at least 2 hours or until firm.

Makes 10 servings

One serving contains: 163 calories, .6g of fat

Fresh Blueberry Crumble

Here the topping and crust are made from the same ingredients and have the same oaty, graham cracker taste. The center is mounded with plump, navy-hued spheres whose natural fruit flavor is enhanced by a sprinkling of cinnamon. It makes a lovely summer pie. And I particularly enjoy the way the blueberries pop when I bite into them and their fresh contents mingle with the other tastes of the pie.

Filling:

3/4 cup sugar

1/2 cup flour

1/2 teaspoon cinnamon

6 cups fresh blueberries (Do not use frozen.)

1 teaspoon lemon juice

Topping:

1 cup vanilla wafer crumbs

1/2 teaspoon cinnamon

1 tablespoon Smart Beat margarine

1. Preheat the oven to 325°F. Lightly coat a 9-inch pie plate with nonstick spray.

2. To make filling: In a large bowl mix the sugar, flour, and cinnamon. Gently fold in the blueberries with a rubber spatula. Pour the filling into the prepared pie plate. Sprinkle with lemon juice and set aside.

3. To make topping: In a small bowl combine the vanilla wafer crumbs, cinnamon, and margarine and stir until well mixed. Sprinkle the topping evenly over the prepared pie.

4. Loosely cover the pie with aluminum foil and poke holes in the foil for venting. Bake for 20 minutes and remove the foil. Bake for an additional 15 minutes.

Makes 10 servings

One serving contains: 157 calories, 1.9g of fat

Sweet Potato Pie

Recreate the tradition of the Old South with this new twist on a classic pie. For those of you who have never tried one it is hard to imagine that sweet potatoes could provide the basis for a delicious pie. Surprisingly, they do, with an effect similar to a uniquely substantial and creamy pumpkin pie. The unusual aspect of this version is the more pervasive bouquet of ginger emanating from the gingersnap crust.

Crust:

1 cup gingersnap cookie crumbs
(about 18 cookies)

2 tablespoons Smart Beat
margarine

Filling:

5 ounces fat-free cream cheese

3 ounces low-fat cream cheese

1 can (14 ounces) fat-free sweetened
condensed milk

2 egg whites

1 egg

2 cups canned yams, drained, or
cooked sweet potatoes, mashed

1/2 teaspoon salt

1/2 teaspoon cinnamon

1/4 teaspoon nutmeg

1/4 teaspoon ginger

1 teaspoon vanilla extract

1. Preheat the oven to 350°F. Coat a 9-inch springform pan with nonstick spray.

2. To make crust: In a small bowl combine the cookie crumbs and margarine. Press into the bottom of the prepared pan and set aside.

3. To make filling: In a large bowl beat together the cream cheeses until smooth. Gradually beat in the condensed milk. Beat in the egg whites and egg. Add the yams, salt, cinnamon, nutmeg, ginger, and vanilla extract and beat until blended.

4. Pour the filling into the prepared crust. Bake for 35 to 40 minutes or until set. Cool on a rack and refrigerate.

Makes 12 servings

One serving contains: 207 calories, 3.9g of fat

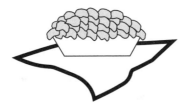

Apricot Dream Pie

Golden hemispheres of apricot add the attractive look of glistening fruit to this thin, creamy pie. The bold, distinctive fruity flavor of the apricot balances nicely the rich, sweet, cream taste of the filling.

Crust:

1 1/4 cups SnackWell's Vanilla Creme Sandwich Cookie crumbs (about 11 cookies)

1 tablespoon Smart Beat margarine

Filling:

1 can (14 ounces) fat-free sweetened condensed milk

1/2 cup light sour cream

2 egg whites

Topping:

16 ounces canned apricot halves, well drained

1/4 cup light apricot preserves, melted

1. Preheat the oven to 375°F. Coat a 9-inch springform pan with nonstick spray and set aside.

2. To make crust: In a small bowl mix together the cookie crumbs and margarine and press into the bottom of the prepared pan.

3. To make filling: In another small bowl, combine the condensed milk, sour cream, and egg whites and mix well. Pour over the prepared crust. Bake for 20 to 25 minutes or until just set. Cool in the refrigerator for 15 minutes.

4. To make topping: Arrange the apricot halves over the cooled pie and brush with melted apricot preserves. Refrigerate until ready to serve and store in the refrigerator.

Makes 10 servings

One serving contains: 219 calories, 3.2g of fat

Sweet Cherry Cream Pie

A thick layer of pink fluffy cherry cream is sandwiched between the crumb topping and pressed crumb crust. The dominant flavor is that of maraschino in a creamy base mixed with crunchy chunks of cherry.

Crust:

1 cup flour

1/2 cup Grape-Nuts

1/4 cup light brown sugar, packed

1/2 cup Smart Beat margarine

Filling:

5 ounces fat-free cream cheese

3 ounces low-fat cream cheese

1/2 teaspoon almond extract

1 cup powdered sugar

1 cup fat-free frozen nondairy whipped topping

1 can (21 ounces) cherry pie filling

1. Preheat the oven to 375°F. Lightly coat a 9-inch pan with nonstick spray.

2. To make crust: In a medium bowl mix together the flour, Grape-Nuts, brown sugar, and margarine until crumbly. Pour the crust mixture into a 13 × 9-inch pan and do not pat it down. Bake for 15 minutes or until golden brown, stirring once during baking.

3. Reserve half the baked crumb mixture for the topping. Firmly press the remaining warm crumb mixture into the bottom and up the sides of the prepared pie pan. Refrigerate for 20 minutes.

4. To make filling: In a small bowl combine the cream cheeses, almond extract, and powdered sugar and blend until smooth. Spread over the cooled, baked crust.

5. In a medium bowl gently mix together with a rubber spatula the whipped topping and cherry pie filling. Spoon over the cream cheese layer. Sprinkle the reserved baked crumb mixture evenly over the pie. Refrigerate for at least 4 hours or overnight.

Makes 12 servings

One serving contains: 212 calories, 2.8g of fat

Blueberry Swirl Pie

This homey pie is cool, fruity, crunchy, and yummy.

Crust:

3/4 cup flour

1/2 cup rolled oats

1/2 cup Grape-Nuts

2 tablespoons sugar

4 tablespoons Smart Beat
margarine, melted

Filling:

1 package (3 ounces) lemon-flavored
gelatin

1/2 cup boiling water

1 can (21 ounces) prepared blueberry pie
filling

1/2 cup fat-free frozen nondairy whipped
topping, thawed

1. Preheat the oven to 400°F. Coat a 9-inch pie pan with nonstick spray.

2. To make crust: In a medium bowl combine the flour, oats, Grape-Nuts, and sugar. Stir in the margarine and mix well. Press the mixture evenly into the bottom and up the sides of the prepared pie pan. Bake for 12 to 15 minutes or until golden brown. Cool.

3. To make filling: In a medium bowl dissolve the gelatin in the boiling water. Stir in the pie filling. Chill until thickened.

4. Pour the filling into the prepared crust. Spoon the whipped topping evenly onto the filling. Swirl the whipped topping into the filling by cutting through the whipped topping with a knife or spatula and lightly folding the topping into the filling to make swirls. Chill in the refrigerator.

Makes 12 servings

One serving contains: 174 calories, 1.2g of fat

Fruit and Cream Cheese Pie

This lovely pie is like an oatmeal cookie sandwich with crunchy pineapple preserves in the middle and a layer of light, whipped, sweet cream cheese on top.

Crust:

- 1 cup flour
- 1 cup rolled oats
- 2/3 cup light brown sugar, packed
- 1/2 teaspoon baking powder
- 1/3 cup Smart Beat margarine
- 10 to 12 ounces pineapple preserves

Topping:

- 1/2 cup powdered sugar
- 3 ounces low-fat cream cheese
- 2 tablespoons low-fat milk
- 1 1/2 teaspoons vanilla extract
- 1 3/4 cups fat-free frozen nondairy whipped topping, thawed

1. Preheat the oven to 350°F.

2. To make crust: In a large bowl combine the flour, oats, brown sugar, baking powder, and margarine. Mix until crumbly. Reserve 1 cup of the crumb mixture and set aside. Pat the remainder into the bottom and up the sides of an ungreased 9-inch pie pan.

3. Spread the preserves over the crust. Pat the remaining crust mixture on top of the preserves. Bake for 20 to 25 minutes or until golden brown. Cool.

4. To make topping: In a small bowl combine the powdered sugar, cream cheese, milk, and vanilla extract. Blend until smooth. Fold in the whipped topping. Spoon over the cooled crust. Refrigerate.

Makes 12 servings

One serving contains: 235 calories, 2.4g of fat

Tip: If you use a glass pie pan, heat the oven to 325°F.

Brownie Pie

This is a great pie for kids because there are so many options for decorating it. Of course it has that deep, rich chocolate fudge flavor that both kids and adults love, but I like to involve the kids by having them create interesting designs in the topping. They do this by imbedding various colors of jelly beans, gummy bears, or minimarshmallows to make faces, outline pictures, or write messages. You can also decorate this pie for holidays or special events. For example at Halloween or Thanksgiving you can place fat-free candy corn in the shape of a pumpkin. Have fun with it!

3 egg whites	1 cup sugar
1 tablespoon canola oil	3/4 cup dark brown sugar, packed
1 tablespoon vanilla extract	1 cup flour
3 tablespoons corn syrup	1 cup unsweetened Dutch cocoa
1/2 cup unsweetened applesauce	1 teaspoon baking powder

Frosting:

1 cup powdered sugar	1 teaspoon vanilla extract
1 tablespoon Smart Beat margarine	2 teaspoons low-fat milk

Drizzle:

1 tablespoon fat-free hot fudge sauce

1. Preheat the oven to 350°F. Coat a 9-inch springform pan with nonstick spray and set aside.

2. In a large bowl combine the egg whites, canola oil, vanilla extract, corn syrup, and applesauce with a hand mixer. Add the sugars and mix well. Stir in the flour, cocoa, and baking powder and mix until smooth.

3. Pour the batter into the prepared pan. Bake for 40 to 45 minutes or until set. A toothpick inserted into the pie near the outside edge should come out clean, but the middle of the pie should be somewhat soft. The key to this pie is in the baking. It must be slightly underbaked to give it the fudgy flavor and consistency. Bake it only until the outside of the brownie becomes firm. The inside must still be soft. Overbaking will change the brownie entirely by causing it to become dry and cake-like. Cool and set aside.

4. To make frosting: In a small bowl combine the powdered sugar and margarine and blend until smooth. Stir in the vanilla extract and milk and beat until smooth and spreading consistency. Frost the top of the cooled brownie pie and set aside.

5. To make drizzle: Bring the hot fudge sauce to room temperature before use. For easier spreading you may wish to heat in a microwave oven for 5 to 10 seconds on high power until slightly warm. Drizzle over the top of the frosted pie.

Makes 16 servings

One serving contains: 250 calories, 2.4g of fat

Crumbly Topped Fresh Peach Cobbler

As with most fruit cobblers this is best prepared in the summertime when the fruit is in season. Then well-ripened peaches are juicy and bursting with the sweet fragrance of the orchard. The golden topping gives the cobbler a homey look and its crunchy texture complements the softness of the center.

Filling:

4 cups sliced fresh peaches

1 cup sugar

1/3 cup flour

1 teaspoon cinnamon

Topping:

3/4 cup flour

3/4 cup light brown sugar, packed

1 1/2 teaspoons cinnamon

1/4 cup Smart Beat margarine

1. Preheat the oven to 375°F. Coat a 9-inch square pan with nonstick spray and set aside.

2. To make filling: In a large bowl gently mix together the peaches, sugar, flour, and cinnamon. Use a rubber spatula to keep the peaches intact. Spoon the filling into the prepared pan and set aside.

3. To make topping: In a medium bowl combine the flour, brown sugar, cinnamon, and margarine. Mix until crumbly. Sprinkle over the filling.

4. Bake for 40 to 45 minutes until the topping is golden and the peaches are tender.

Makes 9 servings

One serving contains: 246 calories, 1.1g of fat

Frozen Desserts

These are appropriate on warm summer evenings or after heavy or spicy meals when you are full and a little thirsty yet want something sweet. Heavy pastries require a cup or two of hot coffee and the combination is too much for a well-laden stomach. On the other hand, there always seems to be a little extra room for frozen desserts, and their lightness on the palate really hits the spot.

Frozen Peanut Butter Mousse Pie

Ice-cold, smooth, and rich, it is hard to believe that this pie is not loaded with high-fat ice cream. Its texture is very much like ice cream, and the distinctive flavor and crunch of real peanuts stands out. It is substantial yet light and not overly filling.

Crust:

1 cup graham cracker crumbs

2 teaspoons sugar

1 tablespoon reduced-fat margarine,
   50% less fat, melted
   (I like Fleischmann's.)

Filling:

2 ounces fat-free cream cheese

1 cup powdered sugar

1/3 cup reduced-fat peanut butter
   (25% less fat)

1/2 cup evaporated skim milk

One 8-ounce container (about 3 1/4 cups)
   fat-free frozen nondairy whipped
   topping, thawed

1/4 cup reduced-fat honey peanuts,
   chopped (Planter's Honey Roasted)

1. Preheat the oven to 400°F.

2. To make crust: In a small bowl mix together the graham cracker crumbs, sugar, and margarine. Press the mixture onto the bottom of a 9-inch springform pan. Bake for 8 minutes. Cool and place in the freezer.

3. To make filling: In a large bowl beat the cream cheese until smooth. Blend in the sugar and peanut butter. Slowly add the evaporated milk and mix thoroughly. Gently fold in the whipped topping.

4. Remove the pie shell from the freezer and pour the filling into it. Sprinkle with the chopped peanuts. Freeze until firm.

Makes 12 servings

One serving contains: 161 calories, 3.0g of fat

Tip: To store the pie, cover with plastic wrap and keep in the freezer.

Frozen Mocha Cream Pie

The consistency of this dessert is unusual. It is that of a thick, slightly gooey, frozen whipped cream. It's not quite solid like an ice cream, yet it's substantially heavier than a whipped cream. And if you like the flavor of chocolate and strong coffee, this is the pie for you.

Its appearance is very appealing too. The deep tan color of the filling contrasts splendidly with the sprinkling of dark chocolate on the top.

Crust:

2 cups reduced-fat Oreo cookie crumbs (about 20 cookies)

3 tablespoons Smart Beat margarine

Filling:

4 ounces low-fat cream cheese

4 ounces fat-free cream cheese

1 can (14 ounces) fat-free sweetened condensed milk

2/3 cup fat-free chocolate syrup or topping (Hershey's Hot Fudge is good.)

1 1/2 tablespoons instant coffee, dissolved in 1 tablespoon hot water

1 teaspoon vanilla extract

1 cup frozen nondairy whipped topping, thawed

1. To make crust: In a small bowl mix the cookie crumbs and margarine. Set aside ¾ cup of the mixture for later use as a topping. Press the remaining mixture into the bottom of a 9-inch springform pan. Chill in the refrigerator.

2. To make filling: In a large bowl beat together the cream cheeses until smooth. Beat in the condensed milk, chocolate syrup, coffee mixture, and vanilla extract and mix until smooth. Gently fold in the whipped topping by hand.

3. Spoon the filling into the chilled crust and sprinkle the reserved crust mixture evenly over the top. Freeze for at least 6 hours until firm. Store covered in the freezer.

Makes 12 servings

One serving contains: 250 calories, 4.7g of fat

"Pretty in Pink" Frozen Raspberry Pie

The color of pink bubble gum, this frozen treat is a blend of tart and sweet. With each bite you get a mouthful of crunchy raspberry seeds, providing the feel of fresh fruit. As usual with raspberries, the flavor is very potent.

Crust:

1 cup vanilla wafer crumbs (about 24 cookies)

2 tablespoons Smart Beat margarine

Filling:

4 ounces low-fat cream cheese

4 ounces fat-free cream cheese

1/2 cup sugar

1 1/2 teaspoons vanilla extract

1 can (14 ounces) fat-free sweetened condensed milk

3 tablespoons lemon juice

3 tablespoons orange juice

1 package (12 ounces) frozen unsweetened raspberries, thawed

1 cup light frozen nondairy whipped topping, thawed

1. To make crust: Preheat the oven to 375°F. In a small bowl mix together the vanilla wafer crumbs and margarine. Press into the bottom of a 9-inch springform pan. Bake for 7 minutes. Cool and place in the freezer.

2. To make filling: In a large bowl beat the cream cheeses together until smooth. Add the sugar, vanilla extract, condensed milk, lemon juice, and orange juice. Beat until smooth. Add the raspberries and mix on low speed until blended. Gently fold in the whipped topping by hand.

3. Remove the crust from the freezer and pour the filling into it. Freeze until firm, approximately 6 hours. To store, cover with plastic wrap and freeze.

Makes 12 servings

One serving contains: 215 calories, 4.0g of fat

Frozen Tropical Cheese Pie

This delectable pie looks and tastes different from any other pie. This cold, creamy creation is a pale mint green and the flavor is an unusual and delectable combination of pistachio, pineapple, citrus, and almond. Chunks of pineapple add just the right bit of interest to the texture.

Crust:

1 1/4 cups SnackWell's Vanilla Creme Sandwich Cookie crumbs

1 tablespoon reduced-fat margarine, 50% less fat (Fleischmann's), melted

Filling:

4 ounces low-fat cream cheese

4 ounces fat-free cream cheese

1 can (14 ounces) fat-free sweetened condensed skim milk

2 tablespoons sugar

1/4 cup lime juice

1 package (3.4 ounces) instant pistachio pudding mix

1 can (8 ounces) crushed pineapple, undrained

3/4 teaspoon vanilla extract

1/2 teaspoon almond extract

1 cup light frozen nondairy whipped topping, thawed

1. To make crust: Preheat the oven to 350°F. In a small bowl mix together the cookie crumbs and margarine. Press into the bottom of a 9-inch springform pan. Bake for 6 minutes. Cool in the refrigerator.

2. To make filling: In a large bowl combine the two cream cheeses and beat until smooth. Gradually beat in the condensed skim milk, sugar, lime juice, and pudding mix. Stir in the vanilla extract and almond extract. Gently fold in the whipped topping.

3. Pour the filling into the prepared crust. Freeze until firm (about 4 hours).

Makes 12 servings

One serving contains: 239 calories, 3.9g of fat

Cookies 'n' Cream Ice Cream Pie

This is a creamy, frozen vanilla pudding pie with a dark, rich Oreo cookie crust.

Crust:

1 cup reduced-fat Oreo cookie crumbs

1 tablespoon Smart Beat margarine

Filling:

1 1/2 cups low-fat milk

1 package (3.4 ounces) instant vanilla pudding mix

One 8-ounce container (about 3 1/4 cups) light frozen nondairy whipped topping, thawed

1/2 cup chopped reduced-fat Oreo cookies

1. To make crust: Preheat the oven to 375°F. In a small bowl combine the crumbs and margarine. Press the mixture into the bottom of a 9-inch pie pan. Bake for 8 minutes. Remove from the oven and cool in the refrigerator.

2. To make filling: Pour the milk into a large bowl and add the pudding mix. Beat until well blended, about 2 minutes. Let stand for 5 minutes or until slightly thickened.

3. Fold in the whipped topping and the Oreo cookies. Spoon into the crust. Freeze the pie until firm, about 6 hours or overnight.

Makes 12 servings

One serving contains: 149 calories, 4.8g of fat

Creamsicle Yogurt Pie

You will recognize this taste. The chiming of the ice-cream truck on a warm summer day led to the cold orange and vanilla taste of a creamsicle on a stick—I've replaced the stick with a graham cracker crust.

Crust:

- 1 1/4 cups ground graham cracker crumbs
- 2 tablespoons sugar
- 3 tablespoons Smart Beat margarine, melted

Filling:

- 1 quart fat-free frozen vanilla yogurt (I like Häagen-Dazs or Colombo.)
- 1 can (6 ounces) frozen orange juice concentrate, thawed

1. To make crust: Preheat the oven to 375°F. In a medium bowl mix together the graham cracker crumbs, sugar, and margarine until well blended. Press into the bottom and up the sides of a 9-inch pie pan. Bake for 8 minutes. Cool in the refrigerator.

2. To make filling: In a large bowl combine the yogurt and orange juice concentrate with a hand mixer. Spread into the cooled prepared crust. Freeze until firm, about 6 hours.

Makes 12 servings

One serving contains: 141 calories, 1.4g of fat

Tip: This dessert looks lovely garnished with fat-free or light whipped cream (available in aerosol cans in the refrigerated section of the market) and fresh orange slices.

Chocolate, Coffee, and Toffee Ice Cream Pie

Say this tongue-twister of a pie name three times quickly and you get a gold star. This fabulous pie makes an impressive dessert for a nice dinner party, unexpected guests, or for your kids. You can make it well in advance and store it in the freezer. It does not require a lot of actual working time to prepare, but you have to be around for several hours to complete each step.

Crust:

2 1/2 tablespoons Smart Beat margarine, melted

1 1/4 cups vanilla wafer crumbs

Filling:

1 pint fat-free chocolate ice cream, slightly softened

1/4 cup English Toffee or Heath Bar baking bits (found in the baking section of the market near the chocolate chips)

1 pint fat-free coffee ice cream, slightly softened

1/2 cup fat-free hot fudge ice cream topping (I like Hershey's.)

1 cup light frozen nondairy whipped topping, thawed

1. Lightly coat a 9-inch springform or pie pan with nonstick spray.

2. To make crust: Preheat the oven to 375°F. In a small bowl combine the margarine and vanilla wafer crumbs and mix until blended. Press into the prepared pan. Bake for 8 minutes. Allow to cool in the refrigerator.

3. Spread the chocolate ice cream over the bottom of the cooled prepared pie shell. Sprinkle 2 tablespoons of the toffee bits evenly over the ice cream. Cover with foil and freeze for 1 hour.

4. Spread the coffee ice cream over the toffee bits and drizzle the hot fudge topping over it. Cover and freeze for 1 hour.

5. Decorate the top of the pie with the whipped topping and the remaining 2 tablespoons of toffee bits. Freeze uncovered for 2 hours or until firm. If it is too hard to cut easily, let it stand at room temperature for a few minutes before serving.

Makes 12 servings

One serving contains: 189 calories, 4.7g of fat

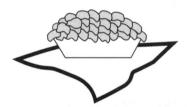

Mud Pie

Like mocha, this ice cream pie is an irresistible combination of chocolate and coffee. It became very popular in the early 1970s and remains a favorite of mine. The name comes, of course, from its looks, presumably, not its taste. It has a dark, rich mahogany color from the hot fudge topping and the chocolate cookie crumb base that sandwich in the chestnut-colored ice cream center.

Crust:

- 1 1/2 cups reduced-fat Oreo cookie crumbs
- 2 tablespoons Smart Beat margarine, melted

Filling:

- 2 pints low-fat Häagen-Dazs coffee fudge ice cream, softened

Topping:

- 1 1/2 tablespoons minichocolate chips
- 1/4 cup fat-free hot fudge sauce, warmed

1. To make crust: Preheat the oven to 350°F. In a medium bowl combine the cookie crumbs and margarine and stir until blended. Press into the bottom of a 9-inch pie pan. Bake for 8 minutes, cool, and set aside in the refrigerator.

2. To make filling: Spread the ice cream on the prepared, cooled cookie crust.

3. Sprinkle the chocolate chips on top. Drizzle the hot fudge sauce over the chips. Place in the freezer until firm, about 6 hours.

Makes 12 servings

One serving contains: 189 calories, 3.7g of fat

Banana Split Pie with Hot Fudge Sauce

Those were the days, when I could eat banana splits to my heart's content and not gain weight. It has been many years since I dared even think about a banana split, yet here is that familiar taste in an ice cream pie, and low-fat to boot.

Crust:

- 1 1/3 cups reduced-fat Oreo cookie crumbs (about 14 cookies)
- 2 tablespoons Smart Beat margarine

Filling:

- 1 pint fat-free frozen vanilla yogurt (I prefer Häagen-Dazs.)
- 2 bananas, sliced

Topping:

- 1 cup fat-free frozen nondairy whipped topping, thawed
- 2 tablespoons fat-free hot fudge topping (Hershey's), at room temperature
- 1 tablespoon chopped almonds

1. To make crust: Preheat the oven to 350°F. Coat a 9-inch pie pan with nonstick spray and set aside.

2. In a small bowl combine the cookie crumbs and margarine and mix well. Press into the bottom and slightly up the sides of the prepared pan. Bake for 8 minutes and cool in the freezer for 15 minutes.

3. In the cooled pie shell spread a thin layer of the frozen yogurt (about ½ pint). Lay the sliced bananas evenly over the yogurt layer. Cover the bananas evenly with the remaining yogurt.

4. Spread the whipped topping over the yogurt. Drizzle the hot fudge sauce over the whipped topping and sprinkle the chopped nuts on the top. Place in the freezer until firm, about 6 hours. Thaw for 5 minutes before serving for ease of slicing. Store covered in the freezer.

Makes 12 servings

One serving contains: 130 calories, 2.1g of fat

Pineapple Sorbet

I have never liked ordinary pineapple sorbets. They are usually too sweet, and you cannot taste the pineapple enough. Here these problems are solved. A little fresh lemon juice adds just the right amount of "bite," while juice and chunks of fresh pineapple provide abundant flavor from the fruit itself.

1 cup unsweetened pineapple juice

1 1/4 cups superfine sugar

2 cups fresh pineapple, shredded or chopped

3 tablespoons fresh lemon juice

3/4 cup chopped fresh strawberries (optional)

1. Combine the pineapple juice and sugar in a medium saucepan. Heat over a low flame and stir until the sugar is dissolved.

2. Allow to cool, then add the fresh pineapple and lemon juice. Chill the mixture in the refrigerator.

3. Pour the mixture into an ice-cream maker and freeze according to the manufacturer's instructions. When serving, top with fresh strawberries if desired.

Makes 6 servings

One serving contains: 211 calories, .3g of fat

Boysenberry Sorbet

In general boysenberries are expensive, so this sorbet is best made during the summer months when the price of the fresh berries is as close to reasonable as it gets. The look of the sorbet is royal purple, fit for royalty—and only royalty can afford to buy the fresh fruit off-season.

3 1/2 cups fresh boysenberries	1 cup superfine sugar
2 tablespoons plus 1 teaspoon fresh lemon juice	2 egg whites
1 cup ice water	

1. Puree the boysenberries and lemon juice in a blender and set aside.

2. Combine the water and sugar in a medium saucepan and heat over a low flame, stirring, until the sugar is dissolved. Allow to cool.

3. Combine the puree and sugar mixture and mix well.

4. Beat the egg whites to a soft peak. Fold the egg whites into the puree mixture. Pour the mixture into an ice-cream maker and freeze according to the manufacturer's instructions.

Makes 6 servings

One serving contains: 171 calories, .2g of fat

Lemon-Lime Sorbet with Papaya

This is one of the healthiest desserts in this book because all the fresh fruit is loaded with vitamin C. And the combination of tart citrus flavors with sweet papaya is delicious and refreshing.

2 cups water

3/4 cup sugar

1/4 cup fresh lime juice

1/4 cup fresh lemon juice

1/2 teaspoon grated lemon zest

1/2 teaspoon grated lime zest

1 1/2 ripe papayas

1. Combine the water and sugar in a medium saucepan and heat over a low flame, stirring, until the sugar is dissolved. Allow to cool.

2. Stir in the lime juice, lemon juice, lemon zest, and lime zest. Chill the mixture well in the refrigerator.

3. Pour into an ice-cream maker and freeze according to the manufacturer's instructions.

4. Cut the papayas in half lengthwise, remove the seeds, and then cut them crosswise into quarters. Fill the papayas with the sorbet.

Makes 6 servings

One serving contains: 123 calories, .1g of fat

Milkshakes and Other Dessert Drinks

I look forward to these refreshing beverages on particular occasions. They hit the spot on hot days; they perk me up in the late afternoons when my energy level starts sagging; and they make a great substitute for the high-fat ice cream I used to crave after a heavy meal, particularly meals that left me thirsty, such as Chinese food. They also make nutritious and attractive snacks for my kids after school or after dinner, although for my kids I use sugar rather than sugar substitutes.

Regular milkshakes contain ice cream, whole milk, and flavorings blended into a cold, thick, and flavorful beverage that contains loads of fat and sugar. They are great for your palate but terrible for your thighs and your health. My low-fat versions taste as fabulous as the real thing, except they are actually good for you and, as a bonus, do not leave you with the sluggish feeling you get after downing a massive load of fat. These light shakes leave a fresh, delightful aftertaste instead of the filmy coating and thirst that are the usual residues of a high-fat, sugary milkshake.

There are a multitude of recipes for low-fat milkshakes on the market that simply do not work. They are low in fat and equally low in taste. I use a variety of tricks to make these fantastic milkshakes work.

The coldness comes from ice cubes that are ground into a froth by your blender. A tad of buttermilk, low-fat milk, or evaporated skim milk add richness to the milk-based drinks without adding a great deal of fat or calories. In addition to sugar substitutes I often add a small quantity of granulated sugar. This is an important item. If you use sugar substitutes only and try to make your light dessert drinks sufficiently sweet you will have to add so much that your drink will develop an unpleasant aftertaste or just become bitter. My technique is to make the drink as sweet as possible with sugar substitutes and then add real sugar to top it off. This will make the drink taste as sweet as it would have if you had used only sugar, but it will contain nowhere near the calories.

Another trick I use to make some recipes taste extrarich is to include a few spoonfuls of instant pudding mix. This increases the calories somewhat but adds no fat. And finally, I introduce larger amounts than usual of powerful flavorings to compensate for the reduced fat, which carries much of the flavor in normal milkshakes.

Vanilla Milkshake

This is one of my favorites when I am in the mood for something sweet and cold like ice cream after a meal, or I want a snack but do not want to blow my diet. This shake tastes rich and creamy and is very filling.

I know it sounds better to advocate pure vanilla, but in this milkshake, imitation vanilla actually tastes better than real. Vanilla is delicate, and in the absence of fat you need a lot of vanilla to carry the flavor. In high concentrations, pure vanilla starts to taste bitter. In contrast you can add imitation vanilla almost to your heart's content without problem.

1 1/2 cups nonfat milk	4 packages Equal
1/4 cup buttermilk	1 tablespoon sugar
1 1/2 cups ice cubes	1 tablespoon imitation vanilla extract

In a blender combine the milk, buttermilk, ice cubes, Equal, sugar, and vanilla extract and mix for 1 minute or until the ice is completely crushed and the mixture is frothy.

Makes 4 cups

One cup contains: 54 calories, .2g of fat

Optional: To make a vanilla malt, add 2 tablespoons Carnation malted milk. With malted milk one cup contains 70 calories and ½ gram of fat.

Orange Nancy

This is a great summertime thirst quencher. I have called it an Orange Nancy rather than an Orange Julius (which it very closely resembles) because the name "Julius" has already been spoken for.

The two secret sauces in a normal Orange Julius are vanilla and milk solids. The trick of blending orange juice with vanilla was a brilliant idea. The vanilla softens the hard, acidic edge of the orange juice and produces a unique flavor, which is at once fruity and creamy. The milk further softens the blend.

Although this drink can be made equally well with orange juice, I usually like to throw in a whole peeled orange because it contains a great deal of extra fiber and nutrients.

5 packages Equal

2 teaspoons sugar

1 cup orange juice or 1 fresh peeled
   orange

1/2 cup nonfat milk

2 teaspoons vanilla extract

1 1/2 cups ice cubes

In a blender combine the Equal, sugar, orange juice, nonfat milk, vanilla extract, and ice cubes. Blend on high for about 1 minute or until the ice is crushed and the mixture becomes frothy.

Makes 3 cups

One cup contains: 42 calories, .1g of fat

Ice-Blended Mocha

Mocha is, essentially, a mixture of coffee and chocolate. Frosty and cool though it may be on a summer day, ice-blended mocha has become a hot item recently with the rise in popularity of Starbucks and the other posh coffeehouses. It is like a sophisticated, grown-up milkshake where one can get a jolt of caffeine in a refreshing, delicious medium.

The problem with most commercial iced mochas is that they are very high in fat and calories. This version solves the problem for those who look forward to sipping a chilly glass of iced-blended mocha on a hot day.

2 teaspoons instant coffee
   (decaf is OK)

2 1/2 tablespoons chocolate cocoa
   mix (Ghirardelli)

2 tablespoons hot water

2 cups small ice cubes

1/3 cup evaporated skim milk

1 package Equal

Cinnamon for sprinkling on top

Light whipped cream (optional)

1. In a small bowl or cup, mix the coffee, cocoa, and hot water until dissolved.

2. In a heavy-duty blender combine the coffee mixture, ice, skim milk, and Equal and mix until slushy. Pour into a glass and top with the cinnamon and light whipped cream if desired.

Makes 1 serving

One serving contains: 150 calories, 1.5g of fat
With light whipped cream one serving contains: 165 calories, 3.0g of fat

Vanilla Mocha Milkshake

This is a lighter-tasting version of a regular mocha milkshake and will, of course, compellingly attract vanilla lovers. It leaves that lovely clean aftertaste of vanilla and coffee.

3/4 cup nonfat milk

1/4 cup buttermilk

1 tablespoon imitation vanilla extract

2 teaspoons instant coffee (Taster's Choice French Vanilla coffee is great for the vanilla lover.)

2 tablespoons sugar

2 packages Equal

2 teaspoons Carnation malted milk

2 teaspoons instant vanilla pudding mix

1 1/4 cups small ice cubes

In a blender combine all the ingredients and mix until all the ice is crushed and the mixture is smooth and creamy.

Makes 3 cups

One cup contains: 78 calories, .5g of fat

Cookies 'n' Cream Milkshake

Why bother to dunk your Oreo cookies in cold milk? Here the cookies are, in a sense, "predunked." Each sip provides an agreeable proportion of familiar Oreo cookie and vanilla flavors, and the shake itself derives extra body from the ground-up cookies. You hardly know whether to drink it or chew it.

1 1/2 cups nonfat milk

1/2 cup low-fat milk

3 tablespoons instant vanilla pudding mix

5 reduced-fat Oreo cookies

2 packages Equal

1 teaspoon imitation vanilla extract

1 1/2 cups small ice cubes

In a blender combine all the ingredients and mix until the ice is well crushed and the mixture is smooth and creamy.

Makes 4 cups

One cup contains: 138 calories, 2.0g of fat

Chocolate Milkshake

As you may have surmised from the many times I have admitted to being a chocoholic, this shake is my favorite. It is as powerfully chocolate as I can make it, yet still low in fat. The small touches, like a teaspoon of chocolate chips ground into the shake, are what generate the lavish flavor.

1 1/2 cups nonfat milk	5 packages Equal
1/3 cup buttermilk	2 teaspoons sugar
1 1/2 cups small ice cubes	2 tablespoons unsweetened Dutch cocoa
1 tablespoon vanilla extract	1 teaspoon chocolate chips

Combine all ingredients in a blender and mix until the ice is well crushed and the mixture is smooth and creamy.

Makes 4 cups

One cup contains: 81 calories, .9g of fat

Variations:

Chocolate Marshmallow Milkshake

Add ½ cup minimarshmallows to the chocolate milkshake ingredients before blending.

One cup contains: 109 calories, .9g of fat

Chocolate Banana Milkshake

Add ½ ripe banana to the chocolate milkshake ingredients before blending.

One cup contains: 97 calories, .9g of fat

Pistachio Milkshake

This pale green shake looks and tastes unusual. It has that pistachio ice cream flavor that so many people love, and its color is interesting to adults and a lot of fun for the kids.

3/4 cup nonfat milk

2 tablespoons buttermilk

1 teaspoon imitation vanilla extract

1/2 teaspoon almond extract

2 tablespoons instant pistachio
    pudding mix

2 tablespoons sugar

2 packages Equal

2 teaspoons Carnation malted milk

1 1/4 cups small ice cubes

Combine all the ingredients in a blender and mix until the ice is well crushed and the mixture is smooth and creamy.

Makes 3 cups

One cup contains: 73 calories, .3g of fat

Chocolate Mocha Milkshake

This shake tastes very rich, with powerful chocolate and coffee flavors. It makes a satisfying dessert-type treat anytime.

3/4 cup nonfat milk

1/2 cup low-fat chocolate milk

1 tablespoon plus 1 teaspoon unsweetened Dutch cocoa

2 teaspoons imitation vanilla extract

2 teaspoons instant coffee

2 teaspoons instant chocolate pudding mix

2 teaspoons Carnation malted milk

2 tablespoons sugar

2 packages Equal

1 1/4 cups small ice cubes

Combine all the ingredients in a blender and mix until the ice is well crushed and the mixture is smooth and creamy.

Makes 4 cups

One cup contains: 84 calories, .7g of fat

Strawberries 'n' Cream Milkshake

This is a great shake for getting your kids to beg you for more of something that is actually good for them. (In this respect it is different from the chocolate shake, which is simply not too bad for them.) A cheery pink in color, this strawberry shake is loaded with fiber and vitamin C from the berries, and calcium and protein from the nonfat milk. And the mixture of vanilla and strawberry is heavenly.

1 1/4 cups nonfat milk

1/4 cup buttermilk

1 1/2 cups ice cubes

4 packages Equal (for kids this can
be replaced by approximately
6 teaspoons sugar)

2 teaspoons sugar

2 teaspoons imitation vanilla extract

1 cup fresh or frozen unsweetened
strawberries

Combine all the ingredients in a blender and mix until the ice is well crushed and the mixture is smooth and creamy.

Makes 4 cups

One cup (with Equal) contains: 55 calories, .2g of fat
One cup (with sugar) contains: 140 calories, .2g of fat

Banana Royal Shake

This is another of those shakes where you get high nutrition in a form that tastes so good you would swear it is bad for you. Bananas are rich in potassium, while the milk, of course, supplies calcium and protein. As a bonus bananas are great in low-fat shakes because their flavor is pervasive and they make the shake thick and creamy. Blended with a hefty dose of vanilla, the taste is luxurious.

It is best to use bananas that are well ripened, even overripe and mushy, because they are sweeter. If the bananas have reached this stage and you are not ready to use them they can be stored for a couple of weeks in the freezer. Just make sure to put them in a thick freezer bag or wrap them well with plastic wrap.

1 1/2 cups nonfat milk

1/4 cup buttermilk

1 1/2 cups ice cubes

4 packages Equal

2 teaspoons sugar

1 tablespoon imitation vanilla extract

1 ripe banana

In a blender combine all the ingredients and mix until the ice is well crushed and the mixture is smooth and creamy.

Makes 4½ cups

One cup contains: 67 calories, .2g of fat

Variations:

Almond Banana Royal Shake

Add ½ teaspoon almond extract. This does not sound like it would mix well with the bananas and vanilla but you will be pleasantly surprised. The almond flavor is one of the few that can hold its own with the banana and actually adds a hint of maraschino cherry flavor, much like you get when you put a cherry on the top of a banana split.

One cup contains: 67 calories, .2g of fat

Piña Colada Shake

Escape to blue skies, balmy air, azure seas, and swaying palms without leaving home. This shake recalls the familiar flavor of the tropics and time squandered without remorse, Jimmy Buffet, and Margaritaville. Paradoxically it is even nutritious, if you resist the temptation to slip in a slug of rum.

1 can (8 ounces) crushed pineapple, undrained

1 cup nonfat milk

1/2 cup low-fat milk

1 teaspoon coconut extract

1 1/2 teaspoons imitation vanilla extract

4 packages Equal

2 teaspoons sugar

1 1/2 cups small ice cubes

In a blender combine all the ingredients and mix until the ice is completely crushed and the mixture is smooth and creamy.

Makes 5 cups

One cup contains: 65 calories, .5g of fat

Cherries Jubilee Shake

Okay, so there is no flaming top to this shake, but I love the sound of the word Jubilee because it reeks of the festivity and sumptuous foods of the Old South. The lush maraschino cherry flavor blended into a pale ruby froth of icy liquid hits the spot on a hot afternoon or warm summer evening.

1 1/2 cups nonfat milk

1/2 cup low-fat milk

1 1/2 cups frozen dark, sweet
    cherries, pitted

2 tablespoons instant vanilla
    pudding mix

3 packages Equal

1 teaspoon vanilla extract

1/2 teaspoon almond extract

1 1/2 cups small ice cubes

In a blender combine all the ingredients and mix until the ice is crushed and the mixture is smooth and creamy.

Makes 4¾ cups

One cup contains: 94 calories, .5g of fat

Lemon Meringue Milkshake

This shake has the exact flavor of a lemon meringue pie. And it catches you off guard to encounter this taste in a milkshake. In fact it takes a little getting used to, but after a few sips you won't want to put the glass down.

1 1/4 cups nonfat milk

1/2 cup low-fat milk

3 tablespoons instant lemon
    pudding mix

1 tablespoon lemon juice

3 packages Equal

1 1/2 cups small ice cubes

In a blender mix all the ingredients until the ice is completely crushed and the mixture is smooth and creamy.

Makes 4¼ cups

One cup contains: 75 calories, .6g of fat

Boysenberry Smoothie

This royal purple drink is thick, creamy, and has a powerful boysenberry taste. It is full of the tiny, crunchy boysenberry seeds so you will be tempted to drink and chew it at the same time. In fact, as a temporary keepsake, you will discover a few leftover seeds to chew on minutes after the drink has been consumed.

1 cup fat-free frozen vanilla yogurt	2 tablespoons Carnation malted milk
1 cup nonfat milk	3 packages Equal
1 cup frozen boysenberries	1 cup small ice cubes

In a blender combine all the ingredients and mix until the ice is completely crushed and the mixture is smooth and creamy.

Makes 3½ cups

One cup contains: 117 calories, .4g of fat

Strawberry Slush

Here is a fruit salad full of vitamins and fiber served as an appetizing, thick, icy drink. You get a tremendous amount of vitamin C from the strawberries, oranges, and lemons.

1 cup fresh strawberries, green stems removed

1/4 cup sugar or 5 to 6 packages Equal

1/2 cup fresh orange juice

1 tablespoon fresh lemon juice

1/2 cup ice cubes

Puree the strawberries in a blender until smooth. Add the sugar, juices, and ice and puree until the mixture is smooth. Serve immediately.

Makes 2 servings

One serving (with sugar) contains: 149 calories, .3g of fat
One serving (with Equal) contains: 52 calories, .3g of fat

Chocolate Ice Cream Soda

This is a great traditional drink that has somehow gone out of fashion. I can't understand why. It features the splendid flavor of heavy chocolate in a light, frozen drink. Its fun to consume because you can control the richness of each spoonful by deciding how much ice cream to include. The soda water cuts the sweetness of the chocolate and makes the drink lighter than a milkshake.

4 tablespoons fat-free hot fudge topping, at room temperature

4 teaspoons imitation vanilla extract

Soda water

1 pint fat-free chocolate ice cream or yogurt

1. Put 1 tablespoon of fudge topping into each of 4 tall glasses. Add 1 teaspoon of the vanilla extract to each glass. Pour in ½ cup of soda water and stir until blended.

2. Add ½ cup of the ice cream or yogurt. Pour in additional soda water until the glass is full. Drizzle 1 more teaspoon of fudge sauce on the top of each.

Makes 4 servings

One serving contains: 150 calories, 0g of fat

Chocolate Root Beer Float

1/2 tablespoon sugar

1 teaspoon unsweetened Dutch cocoa

1/2 tablespoon hot water

1/4 cup fat-free vanilla frozen yogurt or ice cream

3/4 cup chilled diet root beer

1. In a 6-ounce glass stir together the sugar and cocoa. Stir in the hot water.

2. Add the frozen yogurt. Fill the glass with root beer and stir. Serve immediately.

Makes 1 serving

One serving contains: 82 calories, .2g of fat

Twenty-Five-Calorie Coffee Delight

1 cup hot brewed or instant coffee

1/2 package fat-free, sugar-free cocoa mix

Light whipped cream

1 cinnamon stick

1. Pour the coffee into a cup or heavy mug. Add the cocoa mix and stir.

2. Top with whipped cream and place the cinnamon stick in the coffee.

Makes 1 serving

One serving contains: 25 calories, 1.0g of fat

Candy

When I was growing up and learning to bake I was intimidated by the idea of making candy. I thought it required some sort of technical skill level beyond that of baking. I had heard that one needed special thermometers, molds, exotic candy-making equipment, and an intimate knowledge of extraordinary production techniques to produce high-quality candy. Although this may well be true for certain candies, like high-grade chocolates and truffles, I found that many candies are a snap to make and naturally low in fat, though by no means low in sugar.

In fact, as a longtime baker I get a particular satisfaction out of making my own personalized candy. Maybe I took baking for granted a little bit because my grandmothers were bakers and I was exposed to the home-baking process so often. I knew that a good amateur could produce wonderful baked goods in her own kitchen. On the other hand, my experience with candy was that it came in wrappers and boxes and could only be bought at stores. The sudden realization that I could actually make these things at home myself was an exciting surprise.

Homemade candy makes an unusual gift. Most of us have given and received home-baked gifts over the years. Because of its rarity, homemade candy makes a delicious, unique, and welcome gift.

The following are a few general tips about making candy:

- The best weather for making candy is on dry, cool days. Humidity, heat, and altitude affect the production process. If, for example, the day is humid, cook the candy to a temperature a couple of degrees higher than recommended by the recipe. If you live at an altitude substantially above sea level, boiling will occur at a lower temperature. You may need to consult an altitude table to determine your boiling point and adjust your recipes accordingly.

- To prevent grainy or crystallized candy make sure to completely dissolve sugar at low heat. Stir in any grains that adhere to the sides of the saucepan. After boiling the candy do not stir it until it has cooled. Scraping the pan or stirring the candy while it is cooling can cause crystals to form.

- Don't expand the size of the recipe, which changes cooking times. Just make another batch.

- Use a good candy thermometer. To test its accuracy place it in boiling water and verify that it reads 212°F. If it differs from that temperature, take this difference into account when you measure the temperature of your candy during the cooking process.

- When you use the candy thermometer, stand it upright in the candy mixture but do not let it sit on the bottom of the pan. Monitor the rise in temperature carefully. As it moves above 200°F it tends to go up rapidly.

- You can use the cold water test for cooking candy if you don't have a candy thermometer. Here you drop a teaspoonful of the candy mixture into a small bowl of very cold water. You test the hardness of the candy ball with you fingers. If the candy has not reached the desired hardness continue cooking and test again with clean water.

Candy Cooking Tests

HARDNESS TEMPERATURE COLD WATER TEST

Soft Ball (234°F–240°F): Forms a soft ball that flattens when removed from the water.

Firm Ball (242°F–248°F): Forms a firm ball that holds its shape until pressed.

Hard Ball (250°F–268°F): Forms a ball that holds its shape but is pliable.

Soft Crack (270°F–290°F): Separates into hard but not brittle threads.

Hard Crack (300°F–310°F): Separates into hard, brittle threads.

Caramel (320°F–350°F): Do not use the cold water test. Mixture coats metal spoon and forms light caramel-colored mass when poured onto a plate.

Peanut Brittle

Peanuts have one of the most powerful flavors among nuts. So it doesn't take very many of them to give your peanut brittle its characteristic peanut flavor. And since most of this candy's fat is in the peanuts, reducing these to a minimum helps bring the total fat content down to quite a respectable level.

Another way of reducing fat has been to replace every tablespoon of butter called for in a normal recipe with one teaspoon of Smart Beat margarine. Incredibly, the result is a golden crunchy peanut brittle that tastes as good or better than any commercial product, yet has less than one gram of fat per ounce. And stored in an airtight container it lasts for months.

1 1/2 teaspoons baking soda

1 teaspoon water

1 teaspoon vanilla extract

1 1/2 cups sugar

1 cup water

1 cup light corn syrup

3 tablespoons Smart Beat margarine

1/3 cup chopped reduced-fat peanuts
   (Planter's Honey Roasted)

1. Coat 2 cookie sheets with nonstick spray.

2. In a small bowl mix the baking soda, 1 teaspoon water, and vanilla extract and set aside.

3. In a medium saucepan place the sugar, 1 cup water, and corn syrup. Cook over medium heat, stirring occasionally, until 240°F is reached on a candy thermometer or until a small amount of the mixture dropped into very cold water forms a ball that flattens when removed from the water.

4. Stir in the margarine and peanuts. Cook, stirring constantly, until 300°F is reached on a candy thermometer or until a small amount of mixture dropped into very cold water separates into hard, brittle threads. This may take up to 30 minutes. (Be careful not to burn the mixture.)

5. Immediately remove from the heat and quickly stir in the baking soda mixture until light and foamy.

6. Pour half the candy mixture onto each prepared cookie sheet and quickly spread to about ¼ inch thick. Cool and break into pieces.

Makes about 20 ounces

One ounce contains: 114 calories, .6g of fat

Candy

239

Chocolate Peanut Brittle

For those of us who like to mix chocolate with our peanuts, here is a crunchy treat that meets our needs.

1 1/2 teaspoons baking soda

1 teaspoon water

1 teaspoon vanilla extract

1 1/2 cups sugar

1 cup water

1 cup light corn syrup

3 tablespoons Smart Beat margarine

3 tablespoons unsweetened Dutch cocoa

1/3 cup chopped reduced-fat peanuts
   (Planter's Honey Roasted)

1. Coat 2 cookie sheets with nonstick spray.

2. In a small bowl mix the baking soda, 1 teaspoon water, and vanilla extract and set aside.

3. In a medium saucepan place the sugar, 1 cup water, and corn syrup. Cook over medium heat, stirring occasionally, until 240°F is reached on a candy thermometer or until a small amount of the mixture dropped into very cold water forms a ball that flattens when removed from the water.

4. Stir in the margarine, cocoa, and peanuts. Cook, stirring constantly, until 300°F is reached on a candy thermometer or until a small amount of mixture dropped into very cold water separates into hard, brittle threads. This may take up to 30 minutes. (Be careful not to burn the mixture.)

5. Immediately remove from the heat and quickly stir in the baking soda mixture until light and foamy.

6. Pour half the candy mixture onto each prepared cookie sheet and quickly spread to about ¼ inch thick. Cool and break into pieces.

Makes about 20 ounces

One ounce contains: 116 calories, .8g of fat

Peanut Butter Fudge

The inherently powerful aroma of peanuts allows a small amount of reduced-fat peanut butter to dominate the taste of this confection. And since there are times when nothing will satisfy except candy that is excessively sweet and rich, there is a place in anyone's repertoire for these glistening golden tan fudge squares.

2 cups sugar

3/4 cup evaporated skim milk

1/2 teaspoon salt

1 teaspoon vanilla extract

2 tablespoons Smart Beat margarine

6 tablespoons reduced-fat peanut butter (25% less fat)

2 tablespoons reduced-fat honey peanuts (Planter's Honey Roasted), finely chopped

1. Lightly coat a 9-inch square pan with nonstick spray.

2. In a small saucepan combine the sugar, milk, and salt. Over medium heat boil slowly to the soft-ball stage (240°F on a candy thermometer).

3. Turn off the heat and stir in the vanilla extract, margarine, peanut butter, and peanuts. Mix well and pour into the prepared pan. Let cool and cut into squares.

Makes 36 servings

One serving contains: 66 calories, 1.2g of fat

Caramel Apples

Caramel apples are great for kids because they consist mostly of a nutritious apple. The sweet, rich taste of the caramel is the perfect counter to the tartness of the crisp green apple.

I prefer Pippins for caramel apples. The taste of a Pippin by itself is a bit too severe for many people, but the sugary caramel neutralizes the slightly acidic juice and pulp of the apple to produce a treat that is both rich and refreshing. The coating is thin, but it gives the apple the candied and gooey look that is so appealing to children and adults alike. Here a little goes a long way.

1/2 pound caramels, unwrapped

2 tablespoons fat-free sweetened condensed skim milk

3 tablespoons fat-free caramel dessert topping

5 medium green apples

1. In a small saucepan combine the caramels, sweetened condensed milk, and caramel dessert topping. Melt the mixture over low heat, stirring occasionally until it is smooth.

2. Wash the apples and spear each through the stem end with a fork. Dip the apples one at a time into the caramel and spoon more caramel mixture over the apples to coat them completely.

3. Place the dipped apples on a sheet of waxed paper. When they are cooled, chill them in the refrigerator to set the caramel.

Makes 10 servings

One serving contains: 154 calories, 2.1g of fat

Supereasy Microwave Fudge

There are very few things I can make that are this simple yet taste this good. This is a rich, deep chocolate fudge that goes down happily with an ice-cold glass of nonfat milk.

3 3/4 cups powdered sugar

1/2 cup unsweetened Dutch cocoa

1/4 cup evaporated skim milk

2 teaspoons vanilla extract

1/3 cup Smart Beat margarine

1 1/2 tablespoons semisweet mini-M&M baking bits

1. Line an 8-inch square pan with aluminum foil and coat the foil with nonstick spray. Set aside.

2. In a large microwave-safe bowl sift the powdered sugar and cocoa. Stir in the milk and vanilla extract. Top with the margarine. Cook in a microwave on high power for 2 to 3 minutes or until the margarine is melted and the mixture is hot. Spread into the prepared pan.

3. Sprinkle the M&Ms evenly over the top and press gently into the fudge. Refrigerate until firm.

4. Remove from the pan by lifting out the foil and cut into 25 squares. Store in the refrigerator.

Makes 25 servings

One serving contains: 83 calories, .8g of fat

Golden Fudge

Sweet, rich, and loaded with vanilla, this fudge is for vanilla lovers.

1 cup evaporated skim milk

1/2 cup water

1/4 cup light corn syrup

3 tablespoons Smart Beat
  margarine

3 cups sugar

1/2 teaspoon salt

1 teaspoon vanilla extract

1. Line an 8-inch square baking pan with aluminum foil and coat the foil with non-stick spray. Set aside.

2. In a large saucepan combine the milk, water, corn syrup, margarine, sugar, and salt. Cook over medium-high heat, stirring constantly until the mixture comes to a boil. (If sugar crystals are present, wipe down the sides of the pan with a pastry brush dipped in hot water.)

3. Cook while stirring constantly until the mixture reaches the soft-ball stage (238°F on a candy thermometer). Remove from the heat.

4. Without stirring, pour the vanilla extract over the mixture. Leave the thermometer in the pan and allow the mixture to cool to 110°F.

5. Remove the thermometer and with a spoon, stir the mixture for several minutes until it starts to thicken and lose its gloss. Scrape into the prepared baking pan. Refrigerate for 4 hours or until firm.

6. Remove the fudge by lifting the foil out of the pan and cut into 25 squares.

Makes 25 servings

One serving contains: 113 calories, .3g of fat

Peanut Butter Krispies

This tastes similar to the classic marshmallow Rice Krispies bar except it has no marshmallows in it. These have been replaced by the sweetened condensed milk, which provides the required creamy texture. Typical of confections that use peanut butter, its flavor is very powerful.

2/3 cup fat-free sweetened condensed milk

1/4 cup reduced-fat peanut butter (25% less fat)

1/4 cup light corn syrup

1/2 cup light brown sugar, packed

4 cups Rice Krispies

1. Coat a 9-inch square pan with nonstick spray.

2. In a saucepan over medium heat cook the condensed milk, peanut butter, corn syrup, and brown sugar until well mixed and thickened. Stir constantly. Remove from the heat.

3. Quickly stir in the Rice Krispies and mix until coated. (The mixture becomes difficult to handle if you work too slowly.) Pack into the prepared pan.

4. Cool and cut into squares.

Makes 16 servings

One serving contains: 130 calories, 1.5g of fat

Caramel Popcorn

I have eaten a lot of Cracker Jacks over the years because I enjoy them and they are relatively low in fat and calories. This caramel popcorn is, essentially, Cracker Jacks without the peanuts. But you will be surprised at how dramatically the confection improves when it is made fresh at home rather than having spent several months in a box on a shelf. Because of this you will not miss the peanuts.

16 cups popped no-oil or light popcorn

1/4 teaspoon salt

1/2 cup corn syrup

1/3 cup Smart Beat margarine

1/2 cup light brown sugar, packed

1 teaspoon vanilla extract

1. Preheat the oven to 250°F. Line 2 large baking pans with parchment paper or coat with nonstick spray and set aside.

2. Separate the popcorn into two large bowls, equal amounts in each bowl. Sprinkle the salt over the popcorn.

3. In a medium saucepan combine the corn syrup, margarine, and sugar. Cook over medium heat, stirring constantly, until the sugar dissolves. Bring the mixture to a boil and continue boiling for 5 minutes over medium heat, stirring frequently.

4. Remove from the heat, stir in the vanilla extract, and immediately pour over the 2 bowls of popcorn. Stir the popcorn until completely coated.

5. Spread each bowl of popcorn onto a prepared baking pan. Bake 1 hour, stirring every 20 minutes. Cool, remove from the pans, and store in an airtight container.

Makes 16 servings

One serving contains: 92 calories, 1.0g of fat

Marshmallow Popcorn

This is a no-mess, simple recipe that you can make quickly and easily with your kids. It is sticky, gooey, and has a vanilla and caramel flavor.

4 cups popped light or no-oil popcorn

1 cup light brown sugar, packed

1/3 cup Smart Beat margarine

16 large marshmallows

1. Line a baking sheet with parchment paper or coat it with nonstick spray. Set aside.

2. Divide the popcorn evenly into 2 large bowls and set aside.

3. In a medium glass bowl combine the brown sugar and margarine. Microwave for 2 minutes on high power until the margarine is melted. Stir well. Continue microwaving on high for about 3 minutes or until the sugar is dissolved.

4. Add the marshmallows and microwave on high for 2 more minutes or until the marshmallows are melted. Stir well. (The mixture will look foamy.)

5. Pour half the mixture over each bowl of popcorn. Stir until the popcorn is well coated. Spread on the baking sheet until cooled.

Makes 10 servings

One serving contains: 146 calories, 1.2g of fat

Sweet Pastel Popcorn

This is a great treat for the young at heart. The colors are limited only by your imagination. You can tailor them to holidays or for party favors. And they make terrific little gifts when you form them into balls, wrap them in plastic wrap, and tie them with a festive bow.

10 cups popped no-oil or light popcorn

1/2 cup corn syrup

1/3 cup water

1 cup sugar

1/2 teaspoon salt

1/4 cup Smart Beat margarine

1 teaspoon vanilla extract

Food coloring of your choice

1. Line 2 large baking sheets with parchment paper or coat with nonstick spray and set aside. Divide the popcorn evenly into 2 large heat-proof bowls and set aside.

2. In a medium saucepan combine the corn syrup, water, sugar, and salt. Cook over medium heat, stirring constantly, until the sugar dissolves and the mixture comes to a boil. Remove the sugar crystals from the side of the saucepan by frequently washing down the sides with a pastry brush dipped in hot water.

3. Cook until the mixture reaches the hard-ball stage (255°F on a candy thermometer). Remove from the heat. Whisk in the margarine and vanilla extract and stir until completely combined. (The margarine melts almost instantly.)

4. Add the food coloring a few drops at a time until you obtain the desired color. Immediately pour half the hot sugar mixture over 1 bowl of popcorn, stirring until completely coated. Then repeat the process with the other bowl of popcorn and remaining hot sugar mixture.

5. Spread the coated popcorn onto the prepared baking sheets. Cool slightly and shape into balls or clusters.

6. Leave on your counter for a few hours to completely dry or, to speed up the drying process, place in a 200°F oven for about 45 minutes, turning the balls over twice during the drying process.

Makes 10 servings

One serving contains: 162 calories, 1.1g of fat

Microwave Chocolate Caramel Corn

This is a chocolate-lover's twist on classical caramel corn. It is easy to make and delicious.

12 cups popped no-oil or light popcorn

1/4 cup Smart Beat margarine

1/4 cup fat-free sweetened condensed milk

1/4 cup light corn syrup

1/4 cup light brown sugar, packed

1/4 cup sugar

2 1/2 tablespoons unsweetened Dutch cocoa

1 teaspoon vanilla extract

1. Line a baking sheet with parchment paper or coat with nonstick spray and set aside. Divide the popcorn evenly into 2 large bowls and set aside.

2. Place the margarine in a medium, microwave-proof bowl. Cover with a towel and microwave on medium-high power for 20 to 30 seconds or until the margarine is melted.

3. Remove from the microwave and add the condensed milk, corn syrup, sugars, and cocoa. Stir well. Microwave the mixture on high power for 4 minutes, stirring several times. Remove from the microwave and stir in the vanilla extract.

4. Pour half the mixture over each bowl of popcorn and stir to mix well. Cool by spreading on the prepared baking sheet.

Makes 12 servings

One serving contains: 111 calories, 1.1g of fat

Creamy Caramels

2 cups sugar	3/4 cup light corn syrup
2 cups evaporated skim milk	1/2 cup Smart Beat margarine

1. Coat an 8 × 8-inch pan with nonstick spray and set aside.

2. In a medium saucepan combine the sugar, evaporated milk, corn syrup, and margarine. Bring to a boil over medium heat, stirring constantly. Cook, stirring frequently, until 245°F is reached on a candy thermometer or until a small amount of the mixture dropped into very cold water forms a firm ball that holds its shape until pressed.

3. Spread into the prepared pan and cool. Cut into 1-inch squares and wrap each individually in plastic wrap.

Makes 64 caramels

One caramel contains: 44 calories, .3g of fat

Index